2004

A Guide to the Zohar

A

GUIDE

TO THE

ZOHAR

Arthur Green

STANFORD UNIVERSITY PRESS
STANFORD, CALIFORNIA

Stanford University Press
Stanford, California

© 2004 by the Board of Trustees
of the Leland Stanford Junior University.
All rights reserved.

Printed in the United States of America
on acid-free, archival-quality paper

Library of Congress Cataloging-in-Publication Data

Green, Arthur, date–
A guide to the Zohar / Arthur Green.
p.   cm.
Includes bibliographical references.
ISBN 0-8047-4907-8 (cloth)—
ISBN 0-8047-4908-6 (paper)
1. Zohar.   2. Cabala—Early works to 1800.   3. Bible. O.T.
Pentateuch—Commentaries—Early works to 1800.
I. Title.
BM525.A59 G73   2004
296.1'62—dc22   2003021735

Original printing 2004

Last figure below indicates year of this printing:
13   12   11   10   09   08   07   06

Designed by James P. Brommer
Typeset in 11/16 Bembo

For Ebn and Or

אלו יחיו

Contents

Contents   viii

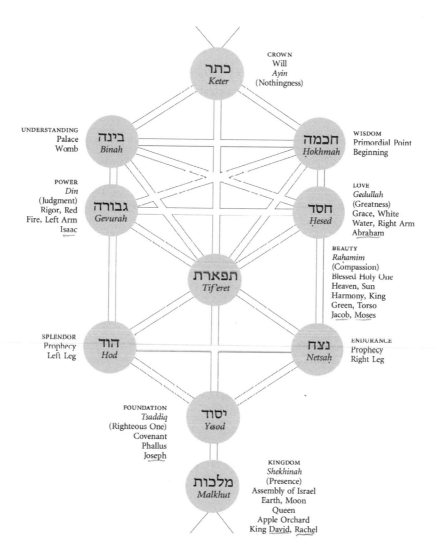

CROWN
Will
Ayin
(Nothingness)

כתר
Keter

UNDERSTANDING
Palace
Womb

בינה
Binah

WISDOM
Primordial Point
Beginning

חכמה
Hokhmah

POWER
Din
(Judgment)
Rigor, Red
Fire, Left Arm
Isaac

גבורה
Gevurah

LOVE
Gedullah
(Greatness)
Grace, White
Water, Right Arm
Abraham

חסד
Hesed

BEAUTY
Rahamim
(Compassion)
Blessed Holy One
Heaven, Sun
Harmony, King
Green, Torso
Jacob, Moses

תפארת
Tif'eret

SPLENDOR
Prophecy
Left Leg

הוד
Hod

ENDURANCE
Prophecy
Right Leg

נצח
Netsah

FOUNDATION
Tsaddiq
(Righteous One)
Covenant
Phallus
Joseph

יסוד
Yesod

KINGDOM
Shekhinah
(Presence)
Assembly of Israel
Earth, Moon
Queen
Apple Orchard
King David, Rachel

מלכות
Malkhut

The Ten Sefirot

Preface

The purpose of this *Guide* is to equip readers, including those who lack prior knowledge of Kabbalah, to understand and appreciate the Zohar text. The *Guide* appears in conjunction with Stanford University Press's publication of *The Zohar: Pritzker Edition*, a new translation by Daniel C. Matt. To appreciate the Zohar in its fullest sense, it must be said, the work needs to be read, indeed carefully studied, in the original. Like most of the kabbalistic tradition within which it stands, the Zohar is fascinated with the mysteries of language, in both its oral and written forms. No reading through the "veil" of translation could do justice to the Zohar's rich and creative appropriation of the nuances of Hebrew and Aramaic speech, its startling transformation of countless biblical verses, and its frequent subtle rereadings of the older rabbinic legacy that together constitute much of the Zohar's charm and genius.

Nevertheless, a great deal can be gained through carefully reading and studying the Zohar in this new translation, which is accompanied by a line-by-line commentary. For this gain to be possible, however, the reader needs to be initiated into the symbolic language in which the work was written. Although the Zohar's poetic spirit often transcends the symbolic conventions, they were always present in the background of the writers' imagination. So too, it was assumed, would they be present in the mind of the reader. The Zohar was composed in the hope that it would be passed on and studied in circles of initiates, as indeed it was for many generations.

Translation of the Zohar into western languages began as early as the fifteenth century, when passages were rendered into Latin for use by Christian devotees of esoteric lore in Renaissance Italy. In the twentieth century, various translations of the entire Zohar, or at least of most sections of it, appeared in German, French, and English. The previous standard English translation is that of Harry Sperling and Maurice Simon, published by the Soncino Press in 1931–34.

The new translation and commentary in the Pritzker Edition of the Zohar bear witness to the high standards of Zohar scholarship that have been achieved in recent decades. These standards are the result of the new attention paid to Kabbalah in academic circles, largely thanks to the writings of Gershom Scholem (1897–1982) and the cadre of scholars he and his successors have trained within the Israeli universities. The first scholar to bring Scholem's approach to kabbalistic studies to North American shores was Alexander Altmann (1906–1987) of Brandeis University, whose students include the current translator of the Zohar, the author of this *Guide*, and indeed a majority of the Kabbalah scholars in the English-speaking world.

To appreciate the Zohar you also need to know something of the historical and literary context in which it appeared. The Zohar makes use of a very wide selection of Jewish texts that preceded it, ranging from the Torah itself to legal, mystical, and philosophical works that were written just shortly before its appearance. It reflects on all of these texts and uses them freely as inspiration for its own unique sort of innovative and sometimes even playful religious creativity. It is also much concerned with the Jews and their history: that recorded in Scripture, the present exile, and the dream of messianic redemption. These too form part of the background needed to understand the Zohar.

The author of this *Guide*, a teacher of Zohar for several decades, invites the reader to join with him in preparing to read this greatest work of the Jewish mystical tradition. For reasons of pedagogy, this

Guide begins with a few matters of definition and then turns to history. We briefly outline the development of Kabbalah in the century leading up to the Zohar, considering also the use made in Kabbalah of prior Jewish sources and the relationship between Jewish philosophy and Kabbalah. We then discuss the essential teachings of Kabbalah, especially the symbolic language of the *sefirot*. With these in place, we turn to the Zohar itself, discussing in turn its style of thought and exegesis, its narrative modes, and the historical context within which it was written. Then we treat some key themes within the Zohar, examining its teachings without, hopefully, reducing them to the object of mere "intellectual history." We proceed to discuss the special sections of the Zohar, its language, and its appearance and authorship. From there we go on to examine the Zohar's canonization and editing, its publication in printed form, and its influence on the later history of Judaism and Jewish mysticism in particular.[1]

The "tall order" detailed in the preceding paragraph requires a disclaimer. Monographs and learned articles have been written on each of the subjects just mentioned. Some of them have been the subject of entire books. This introduction does not seek to break new ground in most of these areas. It is rather a digest of what the writer considers to be the finest scholarship and deepest insights regarding the Zohar that have been written since Scholem began the era of modern Kabbalah scholarship. While responsibility for any misunderstandings or omissions are entirely my own, I wish to acknowledge fully that the insights contained within it are those of three or four generations of scholars

1. The reader who seeks a more extensive introduction to the Zohar should turn to Isaiah Tishby's monumental *Wisdom of the Zohar*. The English translation by David Goldstein (London: Littman Library, 1989) is published in three volumes. Tishby offers a thorough historical analysis of many topics covered by the Zohar, followed by selected passages. Although the original Hebrew version was published in 1949–61 and thus predates much of current Zohar scholarship, Tishby's work remains an invaluable source of knowledge.

who have labored hard as today's *meḥatsdei ḥaqla*, "reapers in the field" of Zohar scholarship. I am grateful to each of them for their contributions to our collective efforts to understand even "a drop in the sea" of the Zohar's profound secrets. Although this *Guide* is written with only minimal footnotes, so as not to burden the reader with scholarly apparatus, references to many of these academic writings (mostly in Hebrew) can be found in the bibliography. The reader is urged to turn from this guide to the Zohar text itself, but also to read the original writings of these scholars, insofar as possible.

A GUIDE TO THE ZOHAR

Part I

INTRODUCTION

I

Prologue

I thank God for not having created me in the   *h ı ce*
period before the Zohar was known to the world,
because the Zohar kept me a Jew.

Rabbi Pinḥas of Korzec (eighteenth century)[1]

The Zohar is the great medieval Jewish compendium of mysticism, myth, and esoteric teaching. It is the central text of the Kabbalah, the grand tradition of Jewish mystical lore that developed in Western Europe in the twelfth and thirteenth centuries. It may be considered the highest expression of Jewish literary imagination in the Middle Ages. The Zohar is also a lush garden of sacred eros, filled to overflowing with luxurious plantings of love between master and disciples; among the mystical companions themselves; between the souls of Israel and *Shekhinah*, God's lovely bride; but most of all between the male and female elements that together make up the Godhead. Revered and canonized by generations of faithful devotees, the Zohar's secret inner universe serves as the basis of kabbalistic faith, both within the boundaries of Judaism and beyond it, to our own day, which has seen a significant revival of interest in Kabbalah and its teachings.

The Zohar is a work of sacred fantasy. To say this about it is by no means to impugn the truth of its insights or to diminish the religious

1. *Imrey Pinḥas ha-Shalem* (Jerusalem: Mishor, 1988), p. 164, #56.

3

profundity of its teachings. The Middle Ages were filled with fantasy. Angels and demons, heavenly principalities, chambers of heaven and rungs within the soul, secret treasures of the spirit that could be seen only by the elect, esoteric domains without end—all of these were found in the writings of Jewish, Christian, and Islamic authors throughout medieval times. All of these descriptions partake of fantasy. It may be said that all theological elaborations, insofar as they are allowed to become pictorial, are fantasy. They depict realities that have not been seen except by the inner eye of those who describe them, or by their sacred sources.

In the case of Judaism, prohibitions derived from the second of the Ten Commandments forbade the depiction of such sacred realms in any medium other than words. Perhaps because of this, the literary imagination became extraordinarily rich. All those creative energies that in other contexts might have sought to reify sacred myth in painting, sculpture, manuscript illumination, or stained glass had instead focused on the word, especially on the timeless Jewish project of commentary and exegesis. In this sense the Zohar may be seen as the greatest work of medieval Jewish *iconography*, but one that exists only in the words of the written page, thence to be distilled in the imagination of its devoted students.

Written in a lofty combination of Aramaic and Hebrew, the Zohar was first revealed to the world around the year 1300. The Castilian Kabbalists who distributed it, orally and in small written fragments, presented it as an ancient text they had recently rediscovered. They claimed it had been composed in the circle of those described within its pages, Rabbi Shim'on ben Yohai and his disciples, who lived in the Land of Israel a thousand years earlier, during the second century of the Common Era. The obscurity of the Zohar's origins combined with its unique language and its rich poetic imagery to lend to the work an aura of unfathomable mystery. While a few of the more critical spirits in each century doubted the Zohar and questioned its authority, the great majority of its readers, and later of Jewry as a whole, believed in the Zohar and venerated it, considering it a holy revelation and a sacred scripture that was to be ranked alongside the Bible and the Talmud as a divinely inspired source of religious truth. Only in modern times, and largely for apologetic reasons, was the Zohar deleted from the canon of what was considered "mainstream" Judaism.

The Zohar is the key text of what is often called *Jewish mysticism*. Before locating the Zohar within the context of the Jewish mystical tradition, we need to turn briefly to the question of mysticism and the multiple ways we use that term when referring to the rich legacy of Judaic materials, stretching from the Bible to the Middle Ages and beyond, to our own day. What do we mean by the term *Jewish mysticism?* The word *mysticism* itself is of Greek and Christian origins and is therefore not native to the traditions of which we speak, none of which saw themselves as "mystical." The equivalent Hebrew terms—*sod* ("secret"), *hokhmah nistarah* ("hidden wisdom"), and *kabbalah* ("tradition")—refer to the esoteric nature of these teachings. *Mysticism* is generally taken to describe primarily a certain category of religious *experiences*, and secondarily all the theology, textual sources, religious movements, and so forth that derive from these experiences. Applying the term *mysticism* to the Zohar or to Jewish sources thus requires some adjustment in its usage and certain reservations about the meanings implied.

Mystics share with other religious people an intense awareness of divine presence and a constant readiness to respond to that presence in both prayer and action. For the mystic, that presence is revealed through powerful and transformative inner experiences. These seem to come from a source that lies beyond the ordinary human mind; they are usually understood as a divine gift, a source of special favor or grace, an act of revelation. The intensity of these experiences lends a sense that the reality they portray represents a deeper source of ultimate truth than do the more usual and widely shared human experiences of sense perception or rational thought.

The experience that lies at the heart of mysticism has been the object of much study and discussion by scholars of religion. Various characteristic types of mystical experience have been outlined and shown to exist across the borders that historically have defined religious traditions and separated them from one another. Mystical experience, whatever its ultimate source, represents a transformation of ordinary human consciousness. Mystics speak of reaching toward another plane of reality. Some of their experiences reflect a slowing down of mental activity to a more restful and contemplative pace; others result from a speeding up of the mind in a rush of ecstatic frenzy. Some mystics describe a fullness of divine presence that overwhelms and floods the mind, while others speak of utter emptiness, a mind that becomes so devoid of content that it can transcend its own existence. There are mystics who see their experiences conveyed by beings outside themselves: God, angels, or heavenly voices speak to them. Others view the experience more internally: a deeper level of the soul is activated, revealing truths or insights that the person was unable to perceive when in an ordinary state of mind. Most of these experiences, as described by those who undergo them, contain some element of striving toward oneness, a breaking down of illusory barriers to reveal the great secret of the unity of all being. The nature of this oneness and its relationship to the phenomenal world that appears before us are described in a great variety of ways, depending on both the personality of the individual mystic and the theology of the tradition out of which he or she speaks.

All of these mystical phenomena as well as others are well represented within the Zohar. The history of Jewish mysticism reveals a variety of experiential types as well as widely differing styles of recording such experiences and integrating them within the normative canon of Jewish religious life. We should bear in mind that in Jewish mysticism, or even within the specific traditions known as Kabbalah, we do not have before us a single linear development of a particular type of mysticism, but rather a variety of mysticisms against the shared background of Judaism, including its sacred texts, its praxis, its interpretive traditions, and the panorama of Jewish history and life experience in the periods under discussion. Even the Zohar itself reflects a panoply of mystical experiences, as is discussed at length in Chapter Six.

Jewish mystical authors are famously shy about speaking directly of their own experiences. This has to do with a longstanding commitment to esotericism with regard to mystical teachings. The second-century Mishnah had already stated that certain matters could be taught only to one student at a time (or "in a whisper," according to another version),[2] while others could be taught only to a single student who was both "wise and understanding of his own accord," seemingly referring to one who had some personal experience of such matters. Written accounts of mystical experience, while they do exist, are relatively rare among the Kabbalists. It is much more their way to garb the personal within the metaphysical, or at the very least to modestly ascribe the experience to one of the ancients rather than to themselves. This is very much the case with the Zohar, as will become clear to the careful reader.

A special problem deserving of mention before we get under way, one that lies at the heart of the specific form of Jewish mysticism called Kabbalah, is that of mysticism and language. The mystic receives insights from a source that is "deeper" or "higher" than the ordinary human mind. But how can those insights be conveyed? Language, whether spoken or written, is our ordinary vehicle of communication, itself a product of the mind and one that shares the limitations of its source. In order to communicate a translinguistic or "ineffable" level of insight, the mystic needs to struggle against the barriers of language,

2. Mishnah Hagigah 2:1; Midrash Tehillim 104:4.

perhaps by stretching the ordinary discursive vehicle to new poetic heights, perhaps by discovering within language a previously untapped symbolic stratum, perhaps by speaking in a holier tongue, by recourse to some code, or else by bearing witness to the utter breakdown of language through such phenomena as glossolalia, sacred stammer, or the glorification of silence.

Judaism offers a distinctive approach to this problem through its ancient belief in the creative and mysterious power of language, stemming back to the myth of creation through the word, the basis of the opening chapter of Genesis. Because of this belief, Jewish mystical sources are filled with reflections on the secrets of language and are often characterized by intense and highly detailed attempts to penetrate inner and hidden levels of speech. Language in general may indeed be a human creation, says the Jewish tradition, but the source of Hebrew, the Holy Tongue, is God. Hebrew is the language of divine speech, that by which God created the world. In some form, though perhaps one hidden to us, that language must have preexisted creation. The Hebrew language as we now have it, seemingly a vehicle of ordinary human speech (though it was seldom spoken among medieval Jews, who used it mainly for the study of sacred writings), bears within it an array of secrets that reveal it to be the premundane language of God. Such a primally charged language, one that offers a key to existence itself, might also be a proper vehicle for the conveying of mystical truth or insights. The nature of God's primordial speech, the question of its relationship to Hebrew as we know it, and the interplay between the language of creation and the languages of revelation and interpretation are all the stuff of kabbalistic discourse, treated frequently within the pages of the Zohar.

2

The Kabbalistic Tradition:
A Brief History Until the Zohar

Jewish mysticism of the Middle Ages is a rereading of earlier Jewish tradition, including both the Bible and the corpus of rabbinic literature. It
has to be understood in the context of the great project of medieval
Jewry as a whole, the interpretation of a received, authoritative, and essentially complete body of normative Jewish teaching. This body of
teaching, canonized in the Geonic age (from eighth to tenth centuries),
nominally commanded the loyalty of all Jewry, with the exception of a
Karaite minority.[1] But the deeper attachment of Jews to this tradition
had to be rewon constantly, especially in the face of both Christian and
Muslim polemics against Judaism, ever the religious culture of a threatened minority living in the shadow of one or the other of its giant off-
spring. Increasingly, various new intellectual currents that came into
fashion among the Jews also occasioned the need for defense or reinterpretation of the tradition. These included Mut'azilite philosophy,[2] Neo-

1. A sect that rejected rabbinic tradition, seeking to live a Judaism based on biblical
authority alone.
2. The earliest form of philosphic rationalism adopted by Jewish thinkers in the
tenth century, based on Islamic models.

9

platonism, and Aristotelianism. The classic form for such reinterpretation of authoritative texts was the commentary, whether on one or more books of the Bible or on a part of the Talmudic legacy. Kabbalah, a new sort of mystical-esoteric exegesis that first appeared in the twelfth century, may be seen as another medieval rereading of the received Jewish canon.

To understand the ways in which Kabbalah, and particularly the Zohar, finds its home within the earlier tradition, we need to distinguish five elements that are present in the legacy that medieval Jews received from the Judaism of the Talmudic age. Although these five are not at all equal either in the amount of text devoted to them or in the degree of formal authority with which they are accredited, each plays an important role in the new configuration of Judaism that Kabbalah represents.

The first of the five elements is *aggadah*, the narrative tradition, contained in the Talmud and the various works of Midrash. Midrash is a hermeneutical term, renderable both as "inquiry" and "homiletics," indicating a way of delving into Scripture that tends toward fanciful and extended rereadings. Much of *aggadah* is legendary in content, expanding biblical history and recreating the biblical landscape in the setting of the rabbinic world. But *aggadah* also includes tales of the rabbis themselves and teachings of wisdom in many forms: maxims, parables, folk traditions, and so forth.

The Kabbalists made great use of the midrashic-aggadic tradition, drawing on both its methods of interpretation and its contents. The hermeneutical assumptions of Midrash—the legitimacy of juxtaposing verses from anywhere within Scripture without concern for dating or context, the rearrangement of words or even occasional substitution of letters, the use of numerology and abbreviation as ways to derive meaning, the endless glorification of biblical heroes and the tarring of villains, and others—were all carried over from Midrash into Kabbalah.

Indeed many of these assumptions were used by other sorts of medieval preachers as well. But the content of the aggadic worldview, with its mythical picture of God as Creator and Divine Ruler who sees everywhere; who acts in history, responds to prayer and human virtue, even suspending the laws of nature to rescue His beloved; who mourns with Israel the destruction of their shared Temple and suffers with them the pain of exile—all this too was faithfully carried over into the kabbalistic imagination. In fact, the Kabbalists were partial to the most highly anthropomorphic and mythical versions of rabbinic tradition, such as those contained in the eighth-century midrashic collection *Pirqei de-Rabbi Eliezer*. Here they stood in sharp contrast to the other emerging intellectual trend of the Middle Ages, Jewish philosophy, which exercised a degree of critical skepticism with regard to the more fantastic claims of the *aggadah* and sought out, whenever possible, those more modest and seminaturalistic viewpoints that could be found among certain of the early rabbis.

The second element is the tradition of *halakhah*, the legal and normative body of Talmudic teaching, the chief subject of study for Jews throughout the medieval era, and thus the main curriculum on which most Kabbalists themselves were educated. The early Kabbalists lived fully within the bounds of *halakhah* and created a meaning system that justified its existence. While later Kabbalah (beginning in the early fourteenth century) contains some elements that are quite critical of *halakhah*, little of this trend is evident in the period before the Zohar. Some transmittors of Kabbalah—Moses Naḥmanides (1194–1270) is the great example—were also active in the realm of halakhic creativity, writing responsa and commentaries on Talmudic tractates. More common was a certain intellectual specialization, undoubtedly reflecting spiritual temperament, spawning Kabbalists who lived faithfully within *halakhah* and whose writings show its patterning of their lives but who devoted their literary efforts chiefly to the realm of mystical exegesis, including kabbalistic comments on the commandments or on aspects of halakhic practice.

A third element of the rabbinic legacy is the liturgical tradition. While liturgical praxis was codified within *halakhah* and thus in some ways is a subset of it, the texts recited in worship, including a large corpus of liturgical poetry, or *piyyut*, constitute a literary genre of their own. Medieval writers, including the mystics of both Spain and Ashkenaz, were much concerned with establishing the precise, proper wording of each prayer. The text of the prayerbook, mostly fixed by compendia dating from the tenth century, became in the Middle Ages the object of commentaries, many of which sought to find their authors' own theologies reflected in these venerated and widely known texts by the ancient rabbis. This is especially true of the Kabbalists, who devoted much attention to the *kavvanah*, or inner meaning, of liturgical prayer. While not formally canonized or seen as the product of divine revelation, as were the books of Scripture, the liturgical texts were regarded as sufficiently holy and mysterious to deserve and require commentary.

The fourth strand of earlier tradition is that of *merkavah* mysticism. *Merkavah* designates a form of visionary mystical praxis that reaches back into the Hellenistic era but was still alive as late as tenth-century Babylonia. Its roots lie close to the ancient Jewish apocalyptic literature, except that here the voyager taken up into the heavens is usually offered a private encounter with the divine glory, one that does not involve metahistorical predictions. Those who "go down into the *merkavah*" sought visions that took them before the throne of God, allowing them to travel through the divine "palaces" (*heikhalot*), realms replete with angels, and at the height of ecstasy, to participate in or even lead the angelic chorus. The term *merkavah* ("chariot") links this tradition to the opening vision of the prophet Ezekiel, which was seen as the great paradigm for all such visionary experiences and accounts. It is also connected to the *qedushah* formula ("Holy, holy, holy is Y-H-W-H of hosts;

the whole earth is filled with His glory!") of Isaiah 6, because it is this refrain that most *merkavah* voyagers recount hearing the angels sing as they stand with them in the heavenly heights.

The *merkavah* tradition was known to the medievals in two ways. Treatises by those who had practiced this form of mysticism, often preserved in fragmentary and inchoate form, were copied and brought from the Near East to western Europe. But just as important were the references to *merkavah* practice in the Talmudic literature itself, which lent legitimacy to the fascination that latter-day mystics clearly felt for this material. Such great Talmudic sages as Rabbi Akiva and Rabbi Yohanan ben Zakkai were associated with *merkavah* traditions. Akiva, considered in some aggadic sources to be a sort of second Moses, is the subject of the most famous of all rabbinic accounts of such mystical voyages.[3] He alone, unlike the other three of the "four who entered the orchard," was able to "enter in peace and leave in peace." While some modern scholars question the historicity of associating the early rabbinic sages with *merkavah* praxis, in the Middle Ages the Talmudic sources were quite sufficient to sustain this link. It was the philosophical questioners of the *merkavah* traditions, rather than their mystical supporters, who were hard-pressed to defend their views. *Merkavah* traditions also had considerable influence on the rabbinic liturgy, and this association also raised their esteem in medieval eyes.

The fifth and final element of this ancient legacy is the hardest to define, partly because it hangs on the thread of a slim body of text, but also because it contains elements that seem contradictory to one another. I refer to the speculative-magical tradition that reached medieval Jewry through the little book called *Sefer Yetsirah* and various other small texts, mostly magical in content, that are associated with it. *Sefer Yetsirah* has been shown to be a very ancient work, close in spirit to aspects of Greek esotericism that flourished in the late Hellenistic era. While the

3. Babylonian Talmud Hagigah 14b.

practice associated with this school of thought is magical-theurgic, even including the attempt to make a *golem*, its chief text contains the most abstract worldview to be found within the legacy of ancient Judaism. By contemplating the core meaning of both numbers and letters, it reaches toward a notion of cosmic unity that underlies diversity, of an abstract deity that serves as cosmic center, in whom (or perhaps better: in which) all being is rooted. The magical praxis is thus a form of *imitatio dei* ("imitation of God"), man's attempt to reignite the creative spark by which the universe has emerged from within the Godhead. Here we have the roots of a theology more abstract than anything to be found in the *aggadah* or the *merkavah* tradition, an essentially speculative and nonvisual mysticism.

Sefer Yetsirah was the subject of a wide variety of commentaries in the Middle Ages, with rationalists as well as mystics claiming it as their own. In the twelfth century, the language and style of thought found in this work became central to the first generations of kabbalistic writing, as reflected by commentaries on it and by the penetration of its terminology into other works as well.

Kabbalah must be seen as a dynamic mix of these five elements, with one or another sometimes dominating. It was especially the first and last elements—the aggadic-mythical element and the abstract-speculative-magical tradition—that seemed to vie for the leading role in forging the emerging kabbalistic way of thought.

Jewish esoteric traditions began to reach the small and isolated communities of Western Europe (some of which dated back to Roman times) perhaps as early as the ninth or tenth century. How these ancient materials first came to Franco-German Jewry is lost in legend, but it is clear from manuscript evidence that much of the old *merkavah* and magical literature was preserved among the earliest Ashkenazic Jews, along with their devotion to both *halakhah* and *aggadah*. These esoteric sources were studied especially by groups in the Rhineland, who added to them their own speculations on God, the cosmos, and the secrets of the Torah. Out of these circles there emerged in the late twelfth and early thirteenth century a movement known to historians as *Hasidut Ashkenaz*, a pietistic revivalism based on small communities or brotherhoods of mystics who committed themselves to high standards of ascetic practice and contemplative devotion. These groups also played a key role in the preservation and further development of esoteric traditions.

It was in the area of southern France called Provence, culturally akin in the High Middle Ages to northern Spain, that a somewhat different version of esoteric speculations began to emerge. These came to be called by the name *Kabbalah*, a term applied to this emerging school of mystical thought in the early thirteenth century. The word means "tradition"; its use in this context indicates that the Kabbalists saw themselves as a conservative element within the Jewish religious community. Their secrets, so they claimed, were *kabbalah*, esoteric teachings received from ancient masters by means of faithful oral transmission from one generation to the next.

The Provencal Jewish community in the twelfth century was one of great cultural wealth, forming something of a bridge between the spiritual legacy of Jewish creativity in Spain of Muslim times and the rather separate world of Jewry in the Ashkenazic or Franco-Rhineish area. Here the great works of Jewish philosophy, including those of Moses Maimonides (1135–1204), were translated into Hebrew, so that a Jewry not conversant with the Arabic original could appreciate them. Provence was a great center of creativity in *halakhah*, religious law, and the ongoing interpretation of the Talmud, which stood at the forefront of intellectual concern among medieval Jews. Traditional homiletics were also cultivated, and important works of Midrash, or homiletical commentary on the Bible, were edited in Provence. But other studies were encouraged as well in this rather "enlightened" atmosphere: Hebrew grammar, biblical exegesis, theology, and poetry all flourished among Provencal Jews. These varied and yet interlinking intellectual traditions were cultivated in small local "houses of study," often dominated by certain families that preserved in their midst ancient oral traditions.

In this cultural area there appeared in about the middle of the twelfth century a previously undocumented sort of theosophical speculation, known in later literature as Kabbalah. The origins of this spiritual and literary movement are obscure and still much debated. There were clearly elements of Near Eastern origin in the earliest Kabbalah, materials related to *merkavah* and late midrashic texts that were present in the Holy Land in the ninth or tenth centuries. There were also strong influences from elements that were to appear in Rhineland Hasidism as well, indicating that at some early point these two movements had a common origin. But here in Provence a new sort of religious discourse began to emerge in circles of mystics who combined knowledge of these various traditions. These groups, which may have been several generations in formation, are known to us as the editors of one of the strangest and most fascinating documents in the long history of Hebrew literature. This slim volume is known as *Sefer ha-Bahir*, awkwardly renderable as *The Book of Clarity*. We first find reference to it in Provencal works of the latter twelfth century, and from that time forward it has a continuous history as a major shaper of Jewish mystical ideas.

The Bahir takes the form of ancient rabbinic Midrash, expounding on biblical phrases, tying one verse of Scripture to another, and constructing units of its own thought around what it offers as scriptural exegesis. It bears a highly distinctive literary style, dialogic in form but highly laconic in presentation. Often the meaning of a passage is difficult to discern, even on the simplest level. Like the old Midrash, it makes frequent use of parables, showing special fondness for those involving kings and their courts, in which God is repeatedly compared to "a king of flesh and blood." In form, then, the Bahir is quite traditional. But as soon as we open its pages to look at the content, we find ourselves confounded:

> Whence do we know that Abraham had a daughter? From the verse "And Y-H-W-H blessed Abraham with *all*" (Gen. 24:1). And it is written: "*All* is called by My name; I created, formed, and made it for My glory" (Is. 43:7). Was this blessing his daughter, or was it perhaps his mother? It was his daughter. To what may this be compared? To a king who had a faithful and perfect servant. He tested him in various ways, and the servant passed all the tests. Said the king: "What shall I do for this servant, or what can I give him? I can only hand him over to my older brother, who may advise him, guard him, and honor him." The servant went to the brother and learned his ways. The elder brother loved him greatly and called him 'beloved': "The seed of Abraham My beloved" (Is. 41:8). He too said: "What can I give him? What can I do for him? I have a beautiful vessel that I have fashioned, containing the most precious pearls, the treasures of kings. I shall give it to him, and he shall attain his place." This is the meaning of "God blessed Abraham with all."[4]

The reader familiar with Midrash (as was the intended audience of the Bahir) will immediately notice something out of the ordinary here. The text simply does not work as Midrash. Questions are asked and not answered, or answered in a way that only adds mystification. An image is proposed, that of the king, which in the context surely refers to God, and suddenly that king turns out to have an elder brother. Abraham's daughter, well known from earlier Midrash, might turn out to be his mother. What sort of questions are these, and what sort of answers? The scholar is almost tempted to emend the text!

If one comes to the Bahir, on the other hand, bearing some familiarity with the methods of mystical teachers, particularly in the Orient,

4. Bahir (ed. Scholem/Abrams), 52.

the text may seem less bizarre. Despite its title, the purpose of the book is precisely to mystify rather than to make anything "clear" in the ordinary sense. Here the way to clarity is to discover the mysterious. The reader is being taught to recognize how much there is that he doesn't know, how filled Scripture is with seemingly impenetrable secrets. "You think you know the meaning of this verse?" says the Bahir to its reader. "Here is an interpretation that will throw you on your ear and show you that you understand nothing of it at all." Everything in the Torah, be it a tale of Abraham, a poetic verse, or an obscure point of law, hints at a reality beyond that which you can attain by the ordinary dialectics of either Talmudic or philosophical thinking.

As we read on in the Bahir, it becomes clear that the authors are not simply advocating obscurantism for its own sake. The text has in mind a notion, often expressed only vaguely, of a world that lies behind the many hints and mysteries of the scriptural word. To say it briefly, the Bahir and all Kabbalists who follow it claim that the true subject of Scripture is God Himself, that revelation is essentially an act of divine self-disclosure. Because most people would not be able to bear the great light that comes with knowing God, the Torah reveals divinity in secret form. Scripture is strewn with hints as to the true nature of "that which is above" and of the mysterious process within divinity that led to the creation of this world. Only in the exoteric, public sense is revelation primarily a matter of divine *will*, teaching the commandments Israel is to follow in order to live the good life. The inner, esoteric revelation is rather one of divine *truth*, a web of secrets pointing to the innermost nature of God's own self.

The earliest documentary evidence of Kabbalah is found in two very different sorts of literary sources. The Bahir constitutes one of these. Alongside it there is a more theoretical or abstract series of kabbalistic writings. These appeared first in the family and close circle of Rabbi Abraham ben David of Posquieres (c. 1125–1198), a well-known

Provencal Talmudic authority. His son, Rabbi Isaac the Blind (d. c. 1235), and others linked to his study circle, including family members, authored brief commentaries on the prayers and on *Sefer Yetsirah*, and disquisitions on the names of God that reflect an ongoing tradition of kabbalistic praxis within their circles. These treatises, quite dry and abstract when compared with the mythical lushness of the Bahir, point to an already quite well defined system of kabbalistic contemplation, suggesting that their appearance after 1150 may reflect a decision to reveal in writing that which had previously been kept secret, rather than an entirely new genre of religious creativity. The rabbinic circles in which Kabbalah was first found were highly conservative; it is hard to imagine them inventing this new sort of religious language on their own. It seems more likely that they saw themselves as guardians and transmittors of a secret tradition, passed down to them from sources unknown, but in their eyes surely ancient.

The context for the publication of the kabbalistic secrets was the great spiritual turmoil that divided Provencal Jewry in the second half of the twelfth century: the controversy over philosophy, and especially over the works of Moses Maimonides. This conflict came to a head with the public burning (by the Dominicans, but possibly with the tacit approval of anti-Maimonidean Jews) of Maimonides' *Guide for the Perplexed* in 1232. The surrounding struggle engaged the intellectual life of the Provencal Jewish elite for several decades. As the era's great halakhic authority and codifier of Jewish law, Maimonides commanded tremendous respect. In many writings of the age he is simply referred to as "the rabbi." But his works raised more than a few questions regarding his degree of theological orthodoxy. Did Maimonides go too far in his insistence that the Bible's ascription of emotions, as well as bodily attributes, to God was a form of anthropomorphism that needed to be explained away? Was it proper that he derived so much of his wisdom from non-Jewish sources, from the Greek and Greco-Islamic philosophical traditions? Was he correct in identifying the ancient rabbinic references to "The Account of the Chariot" and "The Account of Creation" with metaphysics and physics as the philosophers taught them? Did he have a right to dismiss certain old Jewish esoteric speculations as inauthentic nonsense? Still more painful in this law-centered culture: how could the rabbi have given legal status to his own Aristotelian philosophic views, seemingly insisting in the opening section of his Code that any Jew who did not share his views was either an idolator or a naive fool?

But the heart of the Maimonidean controversy went deeper than all of these accusations, touching the very heart of the philosophical notion of the Godhead. Philosophy insisted on divine perfection, on the unchanging, all-knowing, all-capable quality of God. If perfect and unchanging, this God was necessarily self-sufficient and in no need of human actions of any sort. Why then would such a God care about performance of the commandments? How could a Torah centered on religious law, including so much ritual performance, represent the embodiment of divine will? Maimonides taught that indeed God had no "need" for us to fulfill the commandments. The chief purpose of religious observance was educational, a God-given way of cultivating the mind to turn toward God. But once the lesson had been learned, some suspected, there would be those who would come to see the form itself as no longer needed. Moreover, it was rumored that in some circles of wealthy Jewry in Muslim Spain the abstractions of philosophy had begun to serve as an excuse for a more lax view of the commandments and the details of their observance.

Some rabbis of Provence were deeply loyal to a more literalist reading of the Talmudic and midrashic legacy, one that left little room for the radical rationalization of Judaism proposed by the philosophers. Others had been exposed to the esoteric traditions of the Rhineland and northern France, which stood in conflict with the new philosophy partly because they seemed to highlight, rather than minimalize, the anthropomorphic passages in Scripture and tradition. The Franco-Rhineish tradition also had room for a strong magical component to religion. Ancient speculations on the secret names of God and of the angels still held currency in these circles. The use of such names to affect the divine will—utter blasphemy in the eyes of the Maimonideans —was taken for granted in early Ashkenaz, as it had been centuries earlier throughout the Jewish world.

The secrets of Kabbalah were made public in the mid-twelfth century as a way to combat the influence of Maimonidean rationalism. The freedom and implied disinterest in human affairs of the philosophers' God frightened the mystics into coming out of the deep esotericism that until then had restricted them to oral transmission of their teachings within closed conventicles of initiates. Their secrets were to serve as an alternative explanation of the Torah, one that saw Torah and its commandments as not only playing a vital role in the ongoing spiritual life of Israel, but also as having a cosmos-sustaining role in a view of the universe that made them absolutely essential. We will see more of this later when we turn to the actual teachings of the Kabbalists. But it is no accident that two of the key subjects discussed in these earliest kabbalistic speculations are the *kavvanot*, or secret meanings of prayer, and *ta'amey ha-mitsvot*, the reasons for the commandments. Both of these elements are interpreted in a way that insists on the cosmic effectiveness of human actions. The special concentration on divine names played an essential part in early Kabbalah, setting on course a theme that was to be developed over many centuries of kabbalistic praxis.

The secret doctrines first taught in Provence were carried across the Pyrenees in the early thirteenth century, inspiring small circles of mystics in the adjacent district of Catalonia. One key center of this activity was the city of Gerona, well known as the home of two of the most important rabbinic figures of the age, Rabbi Moses ben Naḥman (called Nahmanides) and Rabbi Jonah Gerondi (c. 1200–1263). Naḥmanides, perhaps the most widely respected Jewish intellectual figure of the thirteenth century, is the most important personage associated with the early dissemination of kabbalistic secrets. He was a leading Talmudic commentator, scriptural interpreter, and legal authority. His Torah commentary includes numerous passages—most brief and intentionally obscure, but several lengthy and highly developed—in which he speaks "in the way of truth," referring to secret kabbalistic traditions. Alongside Naḥmanides there emerged a somewhat separate circle of Kabbalists, including two very important teachers, Rabbi Ezra ben Solomon and Rabbi Azriel. These figures seem to have been more innovative than Naḥmanides in their kabbalistic exegesis and also more open to the Neoplatonic philosophy of Abraham Ibn Ezra and others that was gaining credence in their day. Nahmanides was essentially conservative in his kabbalistic readings, insisting that he was only passing down what he had received from his teachers, and his view of philosophical thought in general was quite negative. Rabbi Ezra, the author of commentaries on the Song of Songs and some Talmudic *aggadot*, and his disciple Rabbi Azriel, who wrote a larger treatise on the *aggadot* as well as a widely quoted commentary on the liturgy, combined the legacy of the Bahir with teachings received from Rabbi Isaac the Blind and his nephew Rabbi Asher ben David. They read Kabbalah in a Neoplatonic spirit, which is to say they saw the *sefirot* (discussed shortly) as an ordered series of emanations, increasingly removed from an unknowable primal source.

This Catalonian kabbalistic tradition remained fairly close to the original purpose I have suggested for the publication of kabbalistic secrets. Nahmanides' inclusion of openly kabbalistic references in his highly popular Torah commentary complemented his fierce polemical attacks in that same work on Maimonides' philosophical interpretation

Maimonides

of the Torah. Jacob bar Sheshet, another key Gerona figure, also engaged in the battle against the rationalists. While neither Rabbi Azriel nor Rabbi Ezra of Gerona is known to have written anything outside the realm of Kabbalah, their writings reflect significant rabbinic learning and show them to belong to the same traditionalist and anti-Aristotelian circles. Neoplatonism was a philosophy more amenable to the needs of mystics, they found, thus rediscovering in a Jewish context something that Christian mystics had come to know many centuries earlier.

The fact that a figure of Naḥmanides' prestige had openly associated himself with the publication of kabbalistic teachings undoubtedly did a great deal for the acceptance of this way of thinking in Catalonian and Provencal circles, where his was the leading name in the anti-Maimonidean sector of the rabbinic leadership. Explication of the kabbalistic passages in his commentary became a way of teaching and transmitting secret lore among the students of his leading disciple, Rabbi Solomon ben Adret (c. 1235–c. 1310). Ben Adret himself seems to have been no Kabbalist; his extensive writings consist almost entirely of Talmudic commentaries and responsa to halakhic queries. But his academy provided a setting for the continuance of mystical speculation. Through these circles it was passed on to Rabbi Baḥya ben Asher of Barcelona, a contemporary of the Zohar and perhaps the last great figure of Catalonian Kabbalah.

Around the middle of the thirteenth century, a new center of kabbalistic activity became active in Castile, to the west of Catalonia. Soon the writings of this new group, out of which the Zohar was to emerge, overshadowed those of the earlier Catalonian circle with regard to both volume and originality of output. The Castilian Kabbalists' writings were not characterized by the highly conservative rabbinic attitude that had been lent to Kabbalah by such figures as Rabbi Isaac the Blind and Naḥmanides. This circle's roots were planted more in the Bahir tradition than in the abstract language of early Provencal and Catalonian

Kabbalah. Mythical imagery was richly developed in the writings of such figures as the brothers Rabbi Isaac and Rabbi Jacob ha-Kohen and their disciple Rabbi Moses of Burgos. Their writings show a special fascination with the "left side" of the divine emanation and the world of the demonic.

> R. Isaac ha-Kohen developed a full-blown mythos in which the forces of evil were presented as near autonomous powers emanated in an act of purgation from the depths of divinity. . . . Dependent upon both the divine and the human for their existence, they exist at the liminal outskirts of the Sefirotic realm and the phenomenal universe, at the very borders of chaos and nonbeing. There they wait in ambush for the *Shekhinah* and the worlds which she creates and nurtures. Thus, to the world picture of divine Sefirotic hierarchy and an emanated cosmos, the Castilians add a parallel but antithetical realm of the demonic, serving as the source of all that is destructive in the cosmos.
>
> This conception of the "left hand emanation" is founded on a set of suggestive aggadic statements and Biblical verses. . . . In particular, [the Castilian Kabbalists'] imagination was sparked by . . . R. Abbahu's famous dictum[5]: "The blessed Holy One created and destroyed worlds before He created these, saying: 'These please me. Those did not please me.'" . . . Out of these *aggadot*, R. Isaac spun an elaborate mythos in which the *sefirah binah*, at the dawn of time, welled forth emanations of pure justice, absolute forces of destruction, whose intensity doomed them to almost immediate annihilation. From the residue of these destructive forces rose a hierarchy of powers of pure judgement. Possessing no creative potency of their own, these forces are ontologically dependent upon divinity and are energized by the power released by human transgression.[6]

Because of their fascination with myths of the demonic realm, this group was characterized by Gershom Scholem as the "Gnostic Circle"

5. Midrash Bereshit Rabbah 9:2.
6. Seth Brody, *Cosmos and Consciousness*, chap. 1. The language of this dissertation by my late and much-lamented student has influenced some formulations found elsewhere in this *Guide* as well. I fully acknowledge my indebtedness to him.

of Castilian Kabbalists. Their writings had great influence on the further development of kabbalistic thought. They are the most immediate predecessors of the circle of Kabbalists represented in the Zohar.
The mythical imagination of the Zohar, reaching to its greatest heights
in depicting the realms of evil, has its roots in this setting. It is likely
that Rabbi Moses de Leon, the central figure in both the writing and
the circulation of the Zohar, saw himself as a disciple of these "Gnostic" Kabbalists. Rabbi Todros Abulafia, a Kabbalist who also served as
an important political leader of Castilian Jewry, is another important
link between these two groups. Although significant in their own day,
the writings of the Gnostic circle were mostly forgotten by later generations of Kabbalists and were not printed until Scholem himself re-
trieved them from rare surviving manuscripts.

There is another difference between the Catalonian and the Castilian circles that is especially important for understanding the Zohar's
place in the history of Kabbalah. The earliest Kabbalists were fascinated
with the origins of the sefirotic world, devoting much of their speculation to the highest *sefirot* and to the relationship of those *sefirot* to that
which lies beyond them (see later discussion for further details). They
were also deeply committed to the full unity of the sefirotic world,
even to its circularity, so that the rising of all the *sefirot* to be united
with the highest one was a frequently articulated goal of contemplation. Varied patterns of inner connection in the upper worlds were reflected in the *kavvanot* of prayers and in understandings of ritual commandments, but the ultimate goal of all of these was the full restoration
of the divine unity and the rise of all to the highest rung, designated as
mahashavah or *haskel* ("contemplation" or "intellect"). The situation was
quite different in the Castilian writings. Here the emphasis was placed
not on the highest but on the lower part of the sefirotic world, especially on the relationships between "right" and "left" and "male" and
"female." The counter-balancing of demonic energies needed the

strengthening of the right-hand power of divine love, and this could be awakened by human love of God and performance of the commandments. As these writings developed, it was fascination with the conjugal mysteries, reflected in the joining together of divine male and female, that overwhelmed all other symbolic interests. The uniting of the male sixth and ninth *sefirot* with the female tenth became the chief and in some places the almost unique object of concern and the way of explaining the religious life as a whole. The *mysterium conjunctionis* or *zivvuga qaddisha* lies at the very heart of Zoharic teaching.

In the divergence between these two tendencies within Kabbalah, we see mythical and abstractionist elements struggling within the emerging self-articulation of the mystical spirit. In raising everything to the very heights of the sefirotic world, the Catalonians were voting for abstraction, for a Kabbalah that led the mystic to experience a God not entirely removed from the rarified transpersonal deity of the Jewish philosophers. The Castilians may have incorporated some aspects of Gerona's Neoplatonism, but their spirit was entirely different. Perhaps influenced in part by renewed contact with more mythically oriented Ashkenazic elements, and in part reflecting also the romantic troubador ethos of the surrounding culture, they wrote in a spirit far from that of philosophy. Here we find a strong emphasis on the theurgic, quasi-magical effect of kabbalistic activity on the inner state of the Godhead and on its efficacy in bringing about divine unity and thus showering divine blessing upon the lower world. The Castilians' depictions of the upper universe are highly colorful, sometimes even earthy. The fascination with both the demonic and the sexual that characterizes their work lent to Kabbalah a dangerous and close-to-forbidden edge that undoubtedly served to make it more attractive, both in its own day and throughout later generations.

The emergence of kabbalistic teaching is more complex and obscure than has been described in the preceding paragraphs. The relationship between Kabbalah and certain late forms of midrashic writing is still not entirely clear. The nature and degree of contact between the early Kabbalists and the German Hasidic circles, especially as reflected in the writings of Rabbi Eleazar of Worms (c. 1165–c. 1230), continues to puzzle scholars. The group of abstract mystical writings known as *Sifrei ha-'Iyyun*, or the "Books of Contemplation," fits somewhere into this puzzle, but the precise date and relationship of these writings to other parts of the pre-Zoharic corpus is still debated by scholars. The sources of the highly distinctive school of "prophetic" or "ecstatic" Kabbalah taught by Rabbi Abraham Abulafia (1240–after 1292), while having little connection to the Zohar, would also require treatment in a full picture of the emergence of kabbalistic thought. But this very brief treatment of major schools and themes should suffice to set forth the context out of which the Zohar emerged and within which it is best understood.

The last quarter of the thirteenth century was a period of great creative expansion among the Kabbalists of Castile. The sefirotic Kabbalah as detailed in the works of such well-known figures as Moses De Leon, Todros Abulafia, Joseph Gikatilla, Isaac Ibn Sahula, Joseph ben Shalom Ashkenazi, Joseph Angelet, and Joseph of Hamadan (?), all dating from the period between 1280 and 1310, constitutes a considerable and highly varied body of writing, even leaving aside the Zohar itself. It was within this circle that fragments of a more highly poetic composition, written mostly in lofty and mysterious Aramaic rather than in Hebrew, first began to circulate. These fragments, composed within one or two generations but edited over the course of the following century and a half, are known to the world as the Zohar.

See diagrams, front [handwritten]

3

Teachings of the Kabbalists:
The Ten Sefirot

this is a good symptom of perception of divine, Judaism [handwritten]

Kabbalah represents a radical departure from any previously known version of Judaism, especially in the realm of theology. While Kabbalists remained loyal followers of normative Jewish praxis as defined by *halakhah*, the theological meaning system that underlay their Judaism was entirely reconstructed. The God of the Kabbalists is not the powerful, passionate Leader and Lover of His people found in the Hebrew Bible; not the wise Judge and loving Father of the rabbinic *aggadah*; nor the enthroned King of *merkavah* visionaries. The Kabbalists' God also differs sharply from the increasingly abstract notions of the deity created by Jewish philosophers in the Middle Ages, beginning with Saadia Gaon in the tenth century and culminating with Maimonides, whose work often stands in the background as the object of kabbalistic polemics. The image of God that first appeared in *Sefer ha-Bahir*, to be elaborated by several generations of Kabbalists until it achieved its highest poetic expression in the Zohar, is a God of multiple mythical potencies, obscure entities eluding precise definition but described through a remarkable web of images, parables, and scriptural allusions.

Elusive [handwritten]

Together these entities constitute the divine realm; "God" is the collective aggregate of these potencies and their inner relationship. The dynamic interplay among these forces is the essential myth of Kabbalah, the true inner meaning, as far as its devotees are concerned, both of the Torah and of human life itself.

In describing the God of the Kabbalists as a figure of myth, I mean to say that the fragmented narratives and scriptural interpretations found in the Bahir and in other early kabbalistic writings refer to a secret inner life of God, thus lifting the veil from the ancient Jewish insistence on monotheism and revealing a complex and multifaceted divine realm. In sharp contrast to the well-known ancient adage of Ben Sira[1] ("Do not seek out what is too wondrous for you; do not inquire into that which lies above you"), these writings precisely seek to penetrate the inner divine world and to offer hints to the reader about the rich and complex life to be found there. Of course outright polytheism (like that of the pagan Gnostic groups of late antiquity) is out of the question here at the heart of a medieval Jewry that defined itself through proud and devoted attachment to the faith in divine Oneness. What we seem to discover in the early Kabbalah are various stages of divine life, elements within the Godhead that interact with one another. In the Bahir these potencies interrelate quite freely and mysteriously; a fixed pattern of relationships is somehow vaguely in the background, but not clearly presented. There is one passage, however, undoubtedly determinitive for later Kabbalah, that enumerates the potencies as ten, setting them out as parallel to the ten utterances ("Let there be . . . ")[2] by which God created the world. This passage may be seen as the earliest quasi-systematic presentation

---

1. Famous wisdom teacher, c. 100 B.C.E., purported author of *The Wisdom of Ben Sira* or *Ecclesiasticus*.
2. Mishnah Avot 5:1.

of kabbalistic teaching, and it therefore needs to be quoted at some length:

> What are the ten utterances? The first is supreme crown, blessed be His name and His people. And who are His people? Israel, as Scripture says: "Know that Y-H-W-H is God; it is He who made us and not [consonantally: *L'*] we ourselves" (Ps. 100:3). Read rather: "We are of Aleph [*L'*]"—to recognize and know the One of Ones, united in all His names.
>
> The second: wisdom, as is written: "Y-H-W-H acquired me at the beginning of His way, before His deeds of old" (Prov. 8:22). And there is no "beginning" but wisdom, as it says: "The beginning of wisdom, the fear of Y-H-W-H" (Ps. 110:11).
>
> The third: quarry of the Torah, treasury of wisdom, quarry of God's spirit, hewn out by the spirit of God. This teaches that God hewed out all the letters of Torah, engraving them with the spirit, casting His forms within it. Thus Scripture says: "There is no rock [*tsur*] like our God" (I Sam. 2:2). Read rather, "There is no artisan [*tsayyar*] like our God."
>
> What is the fourth? The fourth is the righteousness of God, His mercies and kindnesses with the entire world. This is the right hand of God.
>
> What is the fifth? Fifth is the great fire of God, of which it says: "Let me see no more of this great fire, lest I die" (Deut. 18:16). This is the left hand of God. . . .
>
> Sixth is the adorned, glorious, delightful throne of glory, the house of the world to come. Its place is engraved in wisdom, as it says: "God said: 'Let there be light' and there was light" (Gen. 1:3). . . .
>
> Did you say "throne"? But we have said[3] that it is the *crown* of God, of which it has been taught "Israel were crowned with three crowns: the crown of priesthood, the crown of kingship, and the crown of Torah which is higher than both." Indeed, there is a priestly crown, above it a royal crown, and the crown of Torah is above them both. To what may this be compared? A king had a precious and fragrant vessel that he loved greatly. Sometimes he places it on his head; these are the *tefillin* [phylacteries] on the head. Sometimes he takes it in his hand, in the

---

3. The reference is to Mishnah Avot 4:13.

knot of *tefillin*. Sometimes he lends it to his son that it might dwell with him. Sometimes it is called his throne, for he takes it in his hand as an amulet, like a throne [cup?].

Seventh are the plains of heaven. And why is it called heaven? For it is round like a head, teaching that there is water on its right and fire on its left, while it is in the center. It is *SHa-Ma-YiM* ("heaven"), from *eSH* ("fire") and *MaYiM* ("water"), bringing peace between them. Along came fire and found on its side the quality of fire; water came and found on its side the quality of water. Thus "He makes peace in His heights" (Job 25:2).

Seventh? But there are only six [referring to the six directions]! But here is the holy palace that bears them all. It is considered two, and thus seventh. What is it? [Like] contemplation is without end or limit, so this place too has neither end nor limit.

The seventh is the cosmic east, whence comes the seed of Israel. For the spine draws from the mind and reaches to the phallus, whence comes the seed. Thus Scripture says: "From the east I will bring your seed" (Is. 43:5). When Israel are good before the Ever-present, "I will bring your seed" and you will have new seed. But when Israel are bad, the seed is from that which has already come into the world, as is written "A generation comes and a generation goes" (Eccles. 1:4). This teaches that it has come already. And what is (Is. 43:5, cont.) "and from the west I shall gather you"? From that place which turns ever toward the west. Why is it called "west" (*ma'arav*)? Because there all the seed is mixed (*mit'arev*). To what may this be compared? To a king's son who had a lovely and modest bride in his chamber. He would take great wealth from his father's house and bring it to her. She would constantly take it all and hide it, mixing it all together. After a time he sought to see what he had gathered and assembled. Thus "and from the west (or 'assemblage') I shall gather you." And what is it? His father's house, since "from the east I will bring your seed," teaching that he brings from the east and sows to the west. Afterwards he gathers in that which he has sown.

What is the eighth? God has a certain righteous one in His world who is beloved to Him because he upholds the entire world. He is its foundation, its sustainer, the one who sates it, causes it to grow, and gives it joy. He is loved and treasured both above and below, considered awesome and grand both above and below, proper and accepted both above and below, the foundation of all souls. You say "foundation of souls" and call him the eighth? But it says: "On the seventh day He rested and was ensouled!" (Ex. 31:17) . . . To what may this be compared? To a king who had seven gardens. In the central garden there was a lovely fountain, coming from a source of living waters. It watered the three to its right and the three to its left. Whenever it did its work or was filled up, all of them rejoiced. They said of it: For our sake it is being filled. It watered them and caused them to grow; they waited quietly for it and it watered all seven. But it says: "From the east I will bring your seed." Was it one of them while it watered them? I should rather say that it watered the heart and afterwards the heart watered them all. . . .

Why is it that you said "eighth"? Because the eight began and ended with it, in the count. But in action it is the seventh. What is it? On it you begin counting the eight days until circumcision. But are they eight [when counting from the first day]? They are only seven! Why then did God say "eight"? Because of the eight human extremities. What are they? Right and left hand, right and left leg, head, trunk, the place of the covenant at the center, and the female partner, his wife. Thus Scripture says: "He will cleave to his wife and they shall be one flesh" (Gen. 2:24). Thus eight, and the days until circumcision parallel these. But these eight are really only seven, since trunk and phallus are one. Thus eight.

What is nine? He said to him: Ninth and tenth are together, one facing the other. One is five hundred years' distance taller than the other. They are two wheel-like beings, one tending toward the north and the other toward the west, reaching down toward the earth below. Why "below"? The last of the seven lands below, the end of God's *Shekhinah*, beneath His feet, of which Scripture says: "The heavens are My throne and the earth My footstool" (Is. 66:1). There is the eternity of the lower world, as it says: "For eternity of eternities" (Is. 34:10). What is "eternity of eternities"? "Eternity" is one, the one that turns toward the west. Second to it is the one that turns toward north. Third is the one below. Third? But you said: "Two wheels of the chariot!" But the end of *Shekhinah* is also an eternity. Thus "eternity of eternities"—One "eternity" and two "eternities"—this makes three.[4]

4. Bahir (ed. Scholem /Abrams), #96–115.

If we try to ask where "God" is in this complex, detailed, and yet somehow entirely vague picture, the answer is not easy. What do we mean by "God"? Is God the One who is seated on the throne? Then "He" must be higher than the sixth entity. But wait—the throne is also the crown! But no, "crown" is the first of these entities! And is it God who is crowned, or Israel? Let us then think of God as the figure at the center, the one from whom all directions lead forth. But that makes "Him" the seventh entity, identical to the palace. How can all these other entities be "higher" than God?

The God of the Bahir is the entire elusive collectivity that emerges from the daring and highly unsystematic group of images that constitutes the book. There is not a God beyond who possesses or uses these powers. They are quite far from the world of divine "attributes" of which the medieval philosophers wrote with such caution and precision, and with which later apologists sought to identify them. Here we have a God who is a mythical universe, a *pleroma*, or fullness of divine powers, to borrow a term from the world of ancient Gnostic religion.

What is being talked about here is a group of divine entities that are called *sefirot* by early kabbalistic sources outside the Bahir. The term originates in *Sefer Yetsirah*, where it refers to the ten primal numbers that, along with the twenty-two letters of the Hebrew alphabet, constitute the "thirty-two wondrous paths of wisdom" or the essential structure of existence. The Bahir's listing of ten such powers (the ninth and tenth seem like something of an afterthought in this list, deriving from the two angels Metatron and Sandalphon, who stand on either side of the divine throne) reflects a stage in its editing when mythical traditions of diverse origins were being organized into a loose system of associations. *Sefer Yetsirah's* ten *sefirot*, along with the ten divine "utterances" of creation, have here been reinterpreted as a framework for this pattern of mythical powers or entities, around which the Kabbalists' theosophic speculations are now ordered.

We cannot fully explicate all of the images to be found in this passage, and to do so would divert us from our task of seeking out the roots of a system that reaches full development only later, in the generation of the Zohar. But it is noteworthy that imagery derived from the natural world is prominent here: gardens, fountains, and parts of the human body are all symbolic of the inner divine entities. Sexual union, impregnation, and birth are clearly alluded to by the bringing of seed to the house of the bride and the gathering of seed "in the west." The text also contains the earliest rather clear Jewish reference to a belief in reincarnation ("the seed is from that which has already come into the world"), later to be a mainstay of kabbalistic faith. These natural symbols combine with elements from the Jewish cult and rabbinic tradition: the three crowns, the divine throne, *tefillin*, and eighth-day circumcision. These too are now diverted from their original meaning to point to some aspect of this mysterious and complex picture of divine inner life.

The non-Bahir writings of early Kabbalah offer a somewhat different picture. Here the term *Ein Sof* begins to appear as a hidden source from which these ten *sefirot* emerge. Originally part of an adverbial phrase meaning "endlessly," *Ein Sof* is used in this context in a nominal sense to designate "the Endless" or "that which is beyond all limits." *Ein Sof* refers to the endless and undefinable reservoir of divinity, the ultimate source out of which everything flows. *Ein Sof* is utterly transcendent in the sense that no words can describe it, no mind comprehend it. But it is also ever-present in the sense of the old rabbinic adage, "He is the place of the world."[5] To say that *Ein Sof* is "there" but not "here" would entirely falsify the notion. Nothing can ever exist outside of *Ein Sof*. It is thus not quite accurate to say that the *sefirot* "emerge" or "come out of" *Ein Sof*. Within the hidden reaches of infinity, in a way that of necessity eludes human comprehension, there stirs a primal de-

5. Midrash Bereshit Rabbah 68:10.

sire, the slightest rippling in the stillness of cosmic solitude. That desire (not a change, the more philosophically oriented Kabbalist hastens to add, but an aspect of reality that has been there forever) draws the infinite well of energy called *Ein Sof* toward self-expression, a becoming manifest or a concretization that begins with the subtlest of steps, moves toward the emergence of "God" as divine persona, manifests its spectrum of energies in the "fullness" of the ten *sefirot*, and then spills over with plentitude to create all the "lower" worlds, including, as its very lowest manifestation, the material universe. The *sefirot* are thus a revelation, a rendering more accessible, of that which has existed in *Ein Sof* all along.

The *sefirot* constitute the subject of nearly all kabbalistic discourse, including that of the Zohar. It is therefore essential that we understand them in their full complexity, including the subtle and often elusive patterns of thought found in discussion of them. Beginning with the Neoplatonist version of Kabbalah, we may view the *sefirot* through either temporal or spatial lenses as stages or rungs in the self-manifestation of the Deity. As stages in an ongoing process of inner divine revelation, the *sefirot* will emerge one after another, each deriving from and dependent upon the one before it. Indeed both temporal and spatial imagery are employed by the Kabbalists. The lower seven *sefirot* are referred to as *days*, each one proceeding behind those that came before it. Spatial imagery abounds in the many diagrams offered by Kabbalists of concentric circles or arrangements of usually circular entities in various patterns of relationship.

But the *sefirot* exist in neither time nor space. They represent an inner divine reality that is prior to these ways of dividing existence, although both are derived from it. The word *sefirah* as *number* represents a high level of metaphysical abstraction. In *Sefer Yetsirah* the *sefirot* seem to be the numerical "building blocks" of reality; the existence of *sefirot* indicates a certain multiplicity or multifacetedness within the divine unity, a tentative "many" within the absolute One. This means that the oneness of God has a dynamic side; it is a one that is not simple and undifferentiated but teeming with energy, life, and passion. There are even tensions and forces that pull in opposite directions within this unity, so that for the Kabbalist *yihud ha-shem*, understood previously as the *proclamation* of the oneness of God, now comes to mean *effecting* the unity of God, bringing the *sefirot* together in harmony so that a single energy may flow through them.

It might be helpful to think of the *sefirot* as the Kabbalist's way of responding to the classic question of all mysticism, one we find addressed in many traditions. "If all is one," the mystic asks, "where do the many come from?" The mystic knows, often describes, and longs to return to a world of complete undifferentiated oneness. In Kabbalah this reality lies essentially beyond description and even transcends any possible account of religious experience. It is called either *Ein Sof* or *ayin*, the realm of primal "nothingness" associated with the first *sefirah* that represents only a stirring of divine will but remains beyond any specific content. At this highest level, Kabbalah has a strong apophatic element, or a mysticism of negative content, parallel to the "emptiness of mind" found in some other mystical languages. But even though *Ein Sof* formally stands beyond both experience and description, the Kabbalist believes that this is absolute reality, the deepest truth toward which he aims. Why, then, does this truth lie so far from ordinary human experience? How is it that we live in a phenomenal world so fraught with division, including the most basic separations of God and world, self and other? If the mystic's unitive vision does represent reality, what is the relationship between that truth and the multifaceted, differentiated world in which we seem to live? And why is it that even the Torah seems to reflect a religious worldview so different from this ultimate mystical truth?

The Kabbalist deals with this question, one that applies to both the origins of reality and its ongoing nature, by means of finesse. Multiplicity begins to arise so subtly within the One that its presence can barely be detected. Nothing is ever added to *Ein Sof*, but it ever so gradually reveals itself to contain an increasingly differentiated reality. The most important symbol of this reality is the discovery of the *sefirot*, the ten within the one. The oneness of God is absolute; it does not begin a series and can be followed by no "two." The "ten" of the *sefirot* does not follow the "one" of God but is contained in it, in the way that mathematical tenths are contained within the whole. The revelation of the tenfold nature of the Godhead is the tale of how the abstract deity of a mystical Neoplatonism came to be manifest as the personified God of biblical-rabbinic tradition, and how that God's creation of the lower universe may be seen as standing within the continuum of the "great chain of being" that ceaselessly flows from the indescribable hidden source, allowing for the existence of all that is.

The tension between the philosphical and mythical aspects of Kabbalah, to which I have alluded, is present in any account one can offer of the sefirotic world. The rationale for the *sefirot* just given places them in the realm of philosophical mysticism, a way of dealing with the abstractness of mystical thought in relation to concrete reality. But this account seems to have rather little to do with the ten *sefirot* of the Bahir in the passage translated earlier. The group of divine potencies described there was a mythical universe built out of reflection on Scripture, on the parables of the rabbis, on typical midrashic wordplays, and on a host of ancient esoteric speculations. Kabbalah can be understood only as a thorough amalgamation of these two very different ways of thinking, with the tension between them never fully resolved. The *sefirot* may in fact be viewed as a way of negotiating between the abstraction of mystical thought and the highly concrete, personified religious language of ancient Judaism. The Zohar's poetic imagination will infinitely enrich the mythical depictions of the sefirotic world, but the system of emanation developed by the Catalonian Kabbalists is also fully in place in the back of its authors' minds. In later Kabbalah this tension between the philosophical and mythical views will take slightly different form, emerging as the ongoing debate over whether the *sefirot* are the "essence" of divinity or merely "vessels" into which the single Deity pours His light and through which it comes to be refracted in seemingly different ways.

We are now ready to trace the pattern of the *sefirot* and the essential symbols associated with them. The description in the following paragraphs does not summarize any particular passage in a single kabbalistic text, but it attempts to offer a summary understanding of the *sefirot* as they were portrayed in the emerging Castilian Kabbalah of the late thirteenth century. Further reflections on the meaning of the sefirotic reality as a whole will be saved for the conclusion of this tracing, when the reader will have a detailed grasp of the system.

The first *sefirah* represents the primal stirrings of intent within *Ein Sof*, the arousal of desire to come forth into the varied life of being. There is no specific "content" to this *sefirah*; it is desire or intentionality, an inner movement of the spirit that potentially bears all content but actually bears none. It is therefore often designated by the Kabbalists as "Nothing." This is a stage of reality that lies between being wholly within the One and the first glimmer of separate existence.

Most of the terms used to describe this rather vague realm are apophatic, describing it negatively. "The air that cannot be grasped" is one favorite; "the hidden light" is another. One pictorial image assigned to this realm is that of the crown: *Keter*, the starting point of the cosmic process. Sometimes this rung of being is referred to as *Keter 'Elyon*, the Supreme Crown of God. This image is derived partly from a depiction of the ten *sefirot* in anthropic form, that is to say, in the image of a human being. Since this personification is of a royal personage, the highest manifestation of the emerging spiritual "body" will be the crown. The Kabbalists also adapted an ancient myth (one that reaches as far back as the era when verbal prayer replaced animal sacrifices) of the daily coronation of God by a diadem of words and letters fashioned out of the prayers of Israel. That crown reaches over the head of God, the highest "place" imaginable. The daily coronation rite, taking place in heaven as well as on earth, is central to ancient *merkavah* traditions, and the position of *Keter* at the head of the *sefirot* reflects the influence of *merkavah* mysticism on Kabbalah. But we should also recall that the more primary meaning of the word *keter* is "circle"; it is from this meaning that the notion of the crown is derived. In *Sefer Yetsirah*, the most ancient document that speaks of *sefirot*, we are told that the *sefirot* are a great circle, "their end tied to their beginning, and their beginning to their end." The circularity of the *sefirot* will be important to us further along in our description.

Out of *Keter* emerges *Hokhmah*, the first and finest point of "real" existence. All things, souls, and moments of time that are ever to be exist within a primal point, at once infinitesimally small and great beyond measure. (Like mystics everywhere, Kabbalists love the language of paradox, a way of showing how inadequate words really are to describe this reality.) The move from *Keter* to *Hokhmah*, the first step in the primal process, is a transition from nothingness to being, from pure potential to the first point of real existence. The Kabbalists are fond of describing it by their own reading of a verse from Job's Hymn to Wisdom: "Wisdom comes from Nothingness" (Job 28:12). All the variety of existence is contained within *Hokhmah*, ready to begin the journey forward. Here we see the subtlety of the inner process used to describe the transition from the undifferentiated oneness of *Ein Sof* to the varied nature of existence. In these first two stages we have gone only from "endlessness" to "nothingness" and thence to an immeasurably small "primal point"—hardly a noticable transition at all. But we have also journeyed from utter undifferentiation of the divine will to the deepest roots of each specific potentially extant being—a very re-markable movement indeed.

But *Hokhmah*, meaning "wisdom," is also the primordial *teaching*, the inner mind of God, the Torah that exists prior to the birth of words and letters. As being exists here in this ultimately concentrated form, so too does truth or wisdom. The Kabbalists are building on the ancient midrashic identification of Torah with primordial wisdom and the midrashic reading of "In the beginning" as "through Wisdom" God created the world. Here we begin to see their insistence that Creation and Revelation are twin processes—existence and language, the real and the nominal—emerging together from the hidden mind of God. As the primal point of existence, *Hokhmah* is symbolized by the *yod*, the smallest of the letters, the first point from which all the other letters will be written. Here all of Torah, the text and the commentary added to it in every generation—indeed all of human wisdom—is contained within a single *yod*. This *yod* is the first letter of the name of God. The upper tip of the *yod* points toward *Keter*, itself designated by the *aleph* or the divine name EHYEH.

This journey from inner divine Nothingness toward the beginning of existence is one that inevitably arouses duality, even within the inner realms. As *Hokhmah* emerges, it brings forth its own mate, called *Binah*, or "contemplation." *Hokhmah* is described as a point of light that seeks out a grand mirrored palace of reflection. The light seen back and forth in these countless mirrored surfaces is all one light, but infinitely transformed and magnified in the reflective process. *Hokhmah* and *Binah* are two *sefirot* that are inseparably linked to one another; each is inconceivable to us without the other. *Hokhmah* is too fine and subtle to be detected without its reflections or reverberations in *Binah*. The mirrored halls of *Binah* would be dark and unknowable without the light of *Hokhmah*. For this reason they are often treated by Kabbalists as the primal pair, the ancestral *Abba* and *Imma*, Father and Mother, the deepest polarities of male and female within the divine (and human) self. The point and the palace are also primal Male and Female, each transformed and fulfilled in their union with one another. The energy that radiates from the point of *Ḥokhmah* is described chiefly in metaphors of flowing light and water, verbal pictures used by the mystics to speak of these most abstract levels of the inner Mind. But images of sexual union are never far behind these; the flow of light is also the flow of seed that fills the womb of *Binah* and gives birth to all the further rungs within the ten-in-one divine structure, the seven "lower" *sefirot*.

The terms *Ḥokhmah* and *Binah* reflect two qualities or stages of inner mental activity, and indeed they may be experienced within the self as two aspects of mind: the first flash of intellect, the creative spark, and the depth of thought that then absorbs the spark, shaping and refining it as it takes it into itself. This is a rendition in terms of mental process of that same image of the "point" and the "palace," showing that the language of Kabbalah may be read simultaneously as a myth of cosmic origins and a description of events within the mystic's mind. *Binah* is thus described by the term *quarry*, the rocky place out of which the letters are hewn forth. *Ḥokhmah*, the flash of intellect, seeks articulation. Itself only the single point of a *yod*, it carves deeply into the mind in quest of "letters" or language through which its truth will be spoken. This primal forming of language, still silent within the mind, carries the self-revealing process of creation a step further in the emergence of cosmos, Torah, and the mystic's own mind. That this should be the case is taken for granted by the Kabbalist, since his mind is a microcosm of that which exists "above" and has been created in such a way as to permit it to both reflect and affect happenings on the cosmic plane.

This first triad of *sefirot* constitutes the most primal and recondite level of the inner divine world. It is a reality that the Kabbalist regularly claims to be quite obscure and beyond human ken, although the many references to *kavvanah* reaching *Keter* and the union of all the *sefirot* with their source tend to undercut such assertions. But in most passages in the Zohar, *Binah* stands as the womb of existence, the jubilee in which all returns to its source, the object of *teshuvah* ("turning," "returning")—in short, the highest object of the religious quest to return to the source. Out of the womb of *Binah* flow the seven "lower" *sefirot*, constituting seven aspects of the divine *persona*. Together these constitute the God who is the object of worship and the One whose image is reflected in each human soul. The divine Self, as conceived by Kabbalah, is an interplay of these seven forces or inner directions. So too is each human personality—God's image in the world. (The Hasidic masters of the eighteenth and nineteenth centuries made much of this psychological aspect of Kabbalah's teachings.) This "holy structure" of the inner life of God is called *raza de-mehemenuta*, the "Mystery of Faith," by the Zohar and has been refined in countless images by Kabbalists through the ages. In other words, "God"(here meaning the God of biblical and rabbinic tradition) was the first Being to emerge out of the divine womb, the primal "entity" that took shape as the endless energies of *Ein Sof* began to coalesce.

These seven *sefirot*, taken collectively, are represented in the spatial domain by the six directions around a center (in the tradition of *Sefer Yetsirah*) and in the realm of time by the seven days of the week, culminating in the Sabbath. Under the influence of Neoplatonism, the Kabbalists came to describe the *sefirot* as emerging in sequence. Again, this sequence does not have to be one of time, as the *sefirot* constitute the inner life of Y-H-V-H, where time does not mean what it does to us. The sequence is rather one of an instrinsic logic, each stage a response to that which comes "before" it. The structure consists of two dialectical triads (sets of thesis, antithesis, and synthesis) and a final vehicle of reception that also energizes the entire system from "below," corresponding to *Keter* at the "upper" end.

First to manifest is *Ḥesed*, the grace or love of God. The emergence of God from hiding is an act filled with love, a promise of the endless showering of blessing and life on all beings, each of whose birth in a sense will continue this process of emerging from the One. This gift of love is beyond measure and without limit; the boundless compassion of *Keter* is now transposed into a love for each specific form and creature that is ever to emerge. This channel of grace is the original divine *shefa*, the bounteous and unlimited love of God. But the divine wisdom also understands that love alone is not the way to bring forth "other" beings and to allow them their place. Judaism has always known God to embody judgment as well as love. The proper balance between these two, ever the struggle of the rabbis themselves (loving the people as well as the law), is a struggle that Jewish sources have long seen as existing in God as well. *Hesed* therefore emerges linked to its own opposite, described both as *Din*, the judgment of God, and *Gevurah*, the bastion of divine power. This is a force that measures and limits love, that controls the flow of *Hesed* in response to the needs, abilities, and deserts of those who are to receive it.

Hesed represents the God of love, calling forth the response of love in the human soul as well. *Hesed* in the mystic's soul is the love of God and of all of God's creatures, the ability to continue this divine flow, passing on to others the gift of divine love. *Gevurah* represents the God we humans fear, the One before whose power we stand in trembling. The Kabbalists saw *Hesed* as the faith of Abraham, described by the prophet as "Abraham who loved Me" (Is. 41:8). Abraham, the first of God's true followers on earth, stands parallel to *Hesed*, the first quality to emerge within God. He is the man of love, the one who will leave all behind and follow God across the desert, willing to offer everything, even to place his beloved son upon the altar for love of God. *Gevurah*, on the other hand, is the God called "fear of Isaac" (Gen. 31:42). This is the divine face Isaac sees when bound to that altar, confronting the God he believes is about to demand his life. Isaac's piety is of a different quality than his father's. Trembling obedience, rather than love, marks his path through life. In the Zohar the "fear of Isaac" is sometimes depicted as a God of terror.

The linking together of *Hesed* and *Gevurah* is an infinitely delicate balance. Too much love and there is no judgment, none of the moral demand that is so essential to the fabric of Judaism. But too much power or judgment is even worse. The Kabbalists see this aspect of the divine and human self as fraught with danger, the very birthplace of evil. *Gevurah* represents the "left" side of the divine as the *sefirot* emerge in humanlike form. The Zohar speaks of a discontent that arises on this "left" side of God.[6] *Gevurah* becomes impatient with *Hesed*, unwilling to see judgment set aside in the name of love. Rather than permitting love to flow in measured ways, *Gevurah* seeks some cosmic moment in which to rule alone, to hold back the flow of love. In this "moment" divine power turns to rage or fury; out of it all the forces of evil are born, darkness emerging from the light of God, a shadow of the divine universe that continues to exist throughout history, sustained by the evil wrought by humans below. Here we have one of the most important moral lessons of Kabbalah: judgment untempered by love brings about evil; power obsessed with itself turns demonic. The force of evil is often referred to by the Zohar as *sitra ahara*, the "other side," indicating that it represents a parallel emanation to that of the *sefirot*. But the origin of the demonic reality that both parallels and mocks the divine is not in some "other" distant force. The demonic is born of an imbalance within the divine, flowing ultimately from the same source as all else, the single source of being.

As mentioned earlier, the Castilian Kabbalists were especially fascinated by this "emanation of the left side." Here as in the ancient apocalyptic and Gnostic writings, the imagination was allowed to bring

6. This is in fact one of several myths of the origin of evil to be found within the Zohar. See Chapter Ten in this book for further discussion.

forth its most fantastic creations. There are times when these writers seem to be describing a truly dualistic universe, one in which the powers of good and evil are pitted against one another in an eternal struggle that will end only with the final redemption. Particularly striking in the Zohar is the imaginative resurrection of monsters and demons that seem strangely like figures from the bestiary of ancient Semitic myth, vanquished by biblical monotheism but still echoing in the poetry of the Psalms, Job, and a few other biblical sources. In the Zohar it almost seems as though these presentiments of terror have been awakened from the sleep of millennia to return and haunt new generations. The mythmaking imagination of the Kabbalists leapt upon the scant materials preserved in these verses and expanded in certain later *Midrashim* to create a powerful and indeed frightening demonic host, one that was to thrive and continue to develop in the minds of later generations of the kabbalistic faithful.

This extremely mythic view of the demonic as a cosmic force does not at all set aside the key role that Judaism has always assigned to human responsibility in the creation of evil. The wicked forces in the universe set out to tempt humans and lead them down the path of transgression, to be sure. But these forces themselves are sustained and nourished by human evil. The more apologetic Kabbalists insist that only the *potential* for evil exists within God (as does all potential), and that the negative forces emerging from the left side have no power at all until humans, beginning with the sin of Adam, turn their own energies in the direction of evil. Just as the righteous, as we shall see more fully later, can unify the *sefirot* and bring blessing upon the world by the concentration of their devotional powers, so can the wicked arouse evil in the cosmos by the misdirection of their own inner forces. This is also to say that evil resides within each human being, as it exists in the cosmos as a whole. Our temptation to do evil is the result of the same imbalance of inner forces that exists within the divine cosmic structure, in

whose image every person is made. Neither God's world nor the human self can do without *Gevurah*, represented in the person by self-re-
straint, strength of character, and the knowledge of how to act appro-
priately in a given situation. But we constantly have to be sure that
enough love and compassion get through these restraints, or else we are
in grave danger of doing harm to the cosmos itself as well as to our
own souls. Anger in particular is frowned upon by the kabbalistic
ethos, which always urges its followers to lean toward the "right" or
Hesed side of the self, making sure that love remains sufficiently strong
and free to flow.

The balance of *Hesed* and *Gevurah* results in the sixth *sefirah*, the center of the sefirotic universe. This configuration ideally represents the
personal God of biblical and rabbinic tradition. This is God seated on
the throne, the one to whom prayer is most centrally addressed. Poised
between the "right" and "left" forces within divinity, the "blessed Holy
One" is the key figure in a central column of *sefirot*, positioned directly
below *Keter*, the divine that precedes all duality. The sixth *sefirah* is represented by the third patriarch, Jacob, also called Israel, the perfect integration of the forces of Abraham and Isaac, the God who unites and
balances love and fear. This is not the Jacob of the biblical stories, we
should add, but an idealized patriarch of the kabbalistic imagination. Already in the older Midrash Jacob is referred to as "the choicest among
the patriarchs," the one whose "bed" was perfect in that all his sons
were included within the holy people. The rabbis speak of God as having a special love for the figure of Jacob, whose "image was engraved on
the Throne of Glory."[7] These mythical depictions of the idealized patriarch are woven together by the Kabbalists to create the figure of God
as *yisra'el saba*, "Israel the Elder," the source of blessing to His descendents, who are identified for all time as "the Children of Israel."

Nonpersonal designations for this sixth *sefirah* include *Tif'eret* ("splen-

7. Babylonian Talmud, Shabbat 146a, Hullin 91b; Bereshit Rabbah 68:12, 82:2.

dor"), *mishpat* ("balanced judgment"), and *emet* ("truth"). The three consonants of *emet* represent the first, middle, and last letters of the alphabet. Truth is stretched forth across the whole of Being, joining the extremes of right and left, *Ḥesed* and *Gevurah*, into a single, integrated personality. Thus is the sixth *sefirah* also described as the central "beam" in God's construction of the universe. Adopting a line from Moses' tabernacle (Ex. 26:28), depicted by the rabbis as reflecting the cosmic structure, Jacob, or the sixth *sefirah*, is called "the central beam, reaching from one end unto the other."

In Jacob, or *Tif'eret*, we reach the synthesis that resolves the original tension between *Ḥesed* and *Gevurah*, the inner "right" and "left," love and judgment. The "blessed Holy One," as a personal God, is also the uppermost manifestation called "Israel," thus serving as a model of idealized human personality. Each member of the house of Israel partakes of this Godhead, Who may also be understood as a totemic representation of His people below. "Jacob" is in this sense the perfect human—a new Adam, according to the sages—the radiant-faced elder extending blessing through the world. This is also the God of *imitatio dei*. In balancing their own lives, Israel imitates the God who stands at the center between right and left, balancing all the cosmic forces. That God knows them and sees Himself in them, meaning that the struggle to integrate love and judgment is not only the great human task but a reflection of the cosmic struggle. The inner structure of psychic life is the hidden structure of the universe; it is because of this that humans can come to know God by the path of inward contemplation and true self-knowledge.

The key dialectical triad of *Ḥesed-Gevurah-Tif'eret* is followed on the kabbalistic chart by a second triad, that of the *sefirot Netsaḥ*, *Hod*, and *Yesod*, arranged in the same manner as those above them. Little that is new takes place on this level of divinity. These *sefirot* are essentially channels through which the higher energies pass on their way into the tenth *sefirah*, *Malkhut* or *Shekhinah*, the source of all life for the lower worlds. Historically speaking, the chart evolved in the period between the Bahir and the Zohar. The mostly undefined seventh and eighth *sefirot*, *Netsah* and *Hod* in classical Kabbalah, are descended from the two angels who occupied the ninth and tenth places in the Bahir passage quoted earlier. These two in turn are medieval expansions of the pair of angels called Metatron and Sandalphon in the older sources, standing in front of and behind the divine throne. As Kabbalah evolved, it became important that *Shekhinah* be the tenth *sefirah*, the "end" or "gateway" of divinity, poised precisely at the transition point between divinity and the lower worlds. To make this happen, the lowest two *sefirot* were "elevated" into side supports of the divine edifice. They represent the two pillars of the cosmic temple or the two thighs (sometimes the testicles) of the divine anthropos.

The only major function assigned to *Netsah* and *Hod* in the kabbalistic sources is that they serve as the sources of prophecy. Moses is the single human to rise to the level of *Tif'eret*, to become "bridegroom of the *Shekhinah*." Other mortals can experience the sefirotic universe only as reflected in the *Shekhinah*, the single portal though which they can enter. (This is the "formal" view of the Kabbalists, though it is a position exceeded by a great many passages in the Zohar and elsewhere.) The prophets other than Moses occupy an intermediate position, receiving their visions and messages from the seventh and eighth *sefirot*, making prophecy a matter of participation in the inner sefirotic life of God.

The ninth *sefirah* represents the joining together of all the cosmic forces, the flow of all the energies above now united again in a single place. In this sense the ninth *sefirah* is parallel to the second: *Hokhmah* began the flow of these forces from a single point; now *Yesod*, as the ninth is called, reassembles them and prepares to direct their flow once again. The life force that flows among and animates the *sefirot* is often

described in metaphors of either light or water, the two primal sub-
stances that best reify free-flowing energy. But when the cosmic forces
are gathered in *Yesod* it bcomes clear that this flow is also to be seen as
male sexual energy, specifically as semen, which the Greek physician
Galen saw as originating in the brain (*Hokhmah*), flowing down through
the spinal column (the central column, *Tif'eret*), into the testicles (*Netsah* and *Hod*), and then into the phallus (*Yesod*). The sefirotic process
thus leads to the great union of the nine *sefirot* above, through *Yesod*,
with the female *Shekhinah*. She becomes filled and impregnated with
the fullness of divine energy and in turn gives birth to the lower worlds,
including both angelic beings and human souls.

The biblical personality associated with the ninth *sefirah* is Joseph,
the only figure regularly described in rabbinic literature as *tsaddiq*, or
"righteous." He is given this epithet because he rejected the wiles of
Potiphar's wife, making him a symbol of male chastity or sexual purity.
The *sefirah* itself is thus often called *tsaddiq*, the place where God is represented as the embodiment of moral righteousness. So too is *Yesod* designated as *berit*, or "covenant," again referring to sexual purity through
the covenant of circumcision.

But there is more than one way to read these symbols. The ninth *sefirah* stands for male potency as well as sexual purity. The Kabbalists res-
olutely insist that these purposes are ideally identical and are not to be
separated from one another. Of course sexual transgression and temptation were well known to them; the circle of the Zohar was quite extreme in its views on sexual sin and on the great damage it could cause
to both soul and cosmos. But the inner world of the *sefirot* was completely holy, a place where no sin abided. Here the flow of male energy
represented only fruitfulness and blessing. The fulfillment of the entire
sefirotic system, especially as seen in Castile, lay in the union of these
two final *sefirot*. *Yesod* is, to be sure, the agent or lower manifestation of
Tif'eret, the true bridegroom of the Song of Songs or the King who

weds the *Matronita, Shekhinah*, the Grand lady of the cosmos. But the fascination with the sexual aspect of this union is very strong, especially in the Zohar, and that leads to endless symbolic presentations of the union of *Yesod* and *Malkhut*, the feminine tenth *sefirah*.

By far the richest network of symbolic associations is that connected with the tenth and final *sefirah*. As *Malkhut* ("kingdom"), it represents the realm over which the King (*Tif'eret*) has dominion, sustaining and protecting her as the true king takes responsibility for his kingdom. At the same time, it is this *sefirah* that is charged with dominion over the lower world; the blessed Holy One's *Malkhut* is the lower world's ruler. The Zohar's frequent designation of her as the *Matronita* (a Latin word in Aramaic garb), Matron or Grand Lady of the cosmos, is its way of ascribing this queenly status. The biblical personage associated with *Malkhut* is David (somewhat surprisingly, given its usual femininity), the symbol of kingship. While *Malkhut* receives the flow of all the upper *sefirot* from *Yesod*, She has a special affinity for the left side. For this reason She is sometimes called "the gentle aspect of judgment," although several Zohar passages paint her in portraits of seemingly ruthless vengeance in punishing the wicked. A most complicated picture of femininity appears in the Zohar, ranging from the most highly romanticized to the most frightening and bizarre.

The last *sefirah* is also called *Shekhinah*, an ancient rabbinic term for the indwelling divine presence. In the early Midrash, the *Shekhinah* was said to dwell in Israel's midst, to follow them into exile, and to participate in their suffering. In the latest phases of midrashic literature there began to appear a distinction between God and His *Shekhinah*, partly a reflection of medieval philosophical attempts to assign the biblical anthropomorphisms to a being less than the Creator. In the medieval Jewish imagination this appelation for God was transformed into a winged divine being, hovering over the community of Israel and protecting them from harm. The Kabbalists identify this *Shekhinah* as the spouse or divine consort of the blessed Holy One. She is the tenth *sefirah*, therefore a part of God included within the divine ten-in-one unity. But She is tragically exiled, distanced from Her divine Spouse. Sometimes She is seen to be either seduced or taken captive by the evil hosts of *sitra ahara*; then God and the righteous below must join forces in order to liberate Her. The great drama of religious life, according to the Kabbalists, is that of protecting *Shekhinah* from the forces of evil and joining Her to the holy Bridegroom, who ever awaits Her. Here one can see how medieval Jews adapted the values of chivalry—the rescue of the maiden from the clutches of evil—to fit their own spiritual context.

In the midrashic tradition, *Shekhinah* identifies with the sufferings of the community of Israel and dwells in their midst. Nevertheless, a clear distinction is maintained between these two. *Shekhinah* is the presence of God; *keneset yisra'el* is the collective body of the Jewish people. Sometimes the "Community of Israel" is indeed depicted as a hypostatic entity, standing in God's presence and engaging in dialogue with Him. But this partner in dialogue is always other than God, representing His earthly beloved. In what was surely their most daring symbolic move, the Kabbalists combined these two figures, blurring the once obvious distinction between the human community of Israel and their divine protector. They claimed that *Shekhinah is* the Community of Israel; *keneset yisra'el* became another term for the tenth *sefirah*. Poised precisely at the border between the divine and the lower worlds, She is at once the this-worldly presentiment of God and a heavenly embodiment of Israel.

The identification of *Shekhinah* and *keneset yisra'el* enabled the Kabbalists to take over the entire midrashic tradition regarding the relationship of God and Israel and to declare it their own. Particularly, the rabbis' reading of the Song of Songs as a love-dialogue between God and Israel was now transformed into the key text to set the poetic stage for depicting the inner unity of God as the love of male and female.

The change made here in the dramatic structure of Jewish faith cannot be overstated. The radical monotheism of the prophets, insisting that YHVH had no consort other than His beloved people, was now set aside in favor of an intradivine romance. The essential relationship that Judaism came to depict was now the "secret of faith," the union of male and female with God. The earthly community of Israel remains God's partner and beloved people, but now He and they (the Kabbalists in particular) share in the task of restoring cosmic oneness, of bringing divine male and female face to face with one another so that the lights might shine throughout the universe, so that the waters of life might flow through Her to nourish and sustain all the worlds below.

As the female partner within the divine world, the tenth *sefirah* came to be described by a host of symbols, derived both from the natural world and from the legacy of Judaism, that are classically associated with femininity. She is the moon, dark on Her own but receiving and giving off the light of the sun. She is the sea, into whom all waters flow; the earth, longing to be fructified by the rain that falls from heaven. She is the heavenly Jerusalem, into whom the King will enter; She is the throne upon which He is seated, the Temple or tabernacle, dwelling-place of His glory. In a most blatantly sexual symbolization, She is *aron ha-berit*, the ark of the covenant, that in which the *berit* or covenant (meaning both the Torah and the circumcised phallus) is contained. The tenth *sefirah* is a passive-receptive female with regard to the *sefirot* above Her, receiving their energies and being fulfilled by their presence within Her. But She is ruler, source of life, and font of all blessing for the worlds below, including the human soul. The Kabbalist sees himself as a devotee of the *Shekhinah*, a spiritual knight of the *Matronita*. She may never be worshiped separately from the divine unity. Indeed, this separation of *Shekhinah* from the forces above was the terrible sin of Adam that brought about exile from Eden. Yet it is only through Her that humans have access to the mysteries beyond.

All prayer is channelled through Her, seeking to energize Her and raise Her up in order to effect the sefirotic unity. The primary function of the religious life, with all its duties and obligations, is to rouse the *Shekhinah* into a state of love.

All realms outside the divine proceed from *Shekhinah*. She is surrounded most immediately by a richly pictorialized host. Sometimes these surrounding beings are seen as angels; other times they are the maidens who attend the Bride at Her marriage canopy. They inhabit and rule over variously described realms or "palaces" of light and joy. The Zohar devotes much attention to describing seven such palaces with names that include "Palace of Love," "Palace of the Sapphire Brick" (alluding to the vision of God in Exodus 24:10), "Palace of Desire," and so forth. The "palaces" (*heikhalot*) of the Zoharic world are historically derived from the remains of the ancient *merkavah* or *heikhalot* mysticism, a tradition that was only dimly remembered by the Zohar's day. In placing the *heikhalot* beneath the *Shekhinah*, the Kabbalists meant to say that the visionary ascent of the *merkavah* mystic was a somewhat lesser sort of religious experience than their own symbolic-contemplative ascent to the heights of the sefirotic universe, an ascent with the *Shekhinah* as She reached into the highest realms.

The energy stored in *Malkhut* reaches forth beyond the realm of divine fullness, through these palaces of light, into the lower worlds. While the inner logic of the Kabbalists' emanational thinking would seem to indicate that *all* beings, including the physical universe, flow forth from *Shekhinah*, the medieval abhorrence of associating God with corporeality complicates the picture, leaving Kabbalah with a complex and somewhat divided attitude toward the material world. The world in which we live, especially for the Zohar, is a thorough mingling of divine and demonic elements. Both the holy imprint of the ten *sefirot* and the frightening structure of multilayered *qelippot*, or demonic "shells," are to be found within it.

Now that we have reviewed the order of the *sefirot* and some of the chief symbols associated with them, we have to go back and ask again what we have just described. What do the Kabbalists believe about the *sefirot*? Are they actual "entities," separate, distinguishable realities on the cosmic plane? Can they be that and yet still be *within* God, as the Kabbalists seem to insist? This is partly a theological question, since the kabbalistic system seems to veer terribly close to polytheism, especially insofar as the existence of the *sefirot* is taken literally. But there is also an important epistemological question here as we seek to understand the nature of the reality that the Kabbalists sought to ascribe to the sefirotic world.

The ambiguous attitude toward the "real" nature of the *sefirot* may be traced back to *Sefer Yetsirah*, that ancient and prekabbalistic source from which the term *sefirah* itself is taken. There the *sefirot* are described by the obscure term *belimah*, which may mean "silence" or "holding back," implying some esoteric reservations about the entire discussion. But *belimah* is read by many kabbalistic interpreters as *beli mah*, an awkward way of saying "without substance," meaning that the *sefirot* exist on some plane other than that of ordinary reality. *Sefer Yetsirah* goes on to describe their existence as that of "a flame joined to a coal," seemingly picturing them as darting flames that leap forth from a burning coal but have no possible existence separate from it.

While some of the earliest Kabbalists indeed had to combat accusations of polytheism, more sophisticated critics of Kabbalah have worried that it is in fact a pantheistic system, one that thoroughly compromises the idea of divine "otherness" that seems characteristic of the earlier Jewish tradition. If *Ein Sof* is without end or limit, all of the *sefirot* must exist within it, making them more like aspects or dimensions of a single reality than substantive stages on any real journey toward multiplicity. But what then of the "lower" worlds, insofar as they too are part of the great chain of emanation that proceeds from the *Shekhi-*

nah? Are not they too part of *Ein Sof,* the endless, undifferentiated single source of life? Are the seeming multiplicities and differentiations of this lower world then somehow less than real? What becomes of the place of evil in a pantheistic universe? What of law and human responsibility in a world in which everything exists in an unbroken continuum with the single selfhood of God?

Kabbalists throughout history, including the circle of the Zohar itself, have had to respond to these challenges, sometimes issued from within their own struggling minds as well as articulated by their opponents. Various views are found in the sources. Some authors, especially in the fifteenth and sixteenth centuries, became quite apologetic about kabbalistic language and sought to combine it with the originally very different discourse of medieval Jewish philosophy. Others, including the authors of the Zohar, were closer to pantheism, but rather inconsistently combined it with aspects of dualistic mythology and insistence on a literalist notion of revelation. The history of Kabbalah reflects an ongoing struggle over these issues, sometimes resulting in highly original and creative attempts at resolving the theological difficulties resulting from a position that straddles an all-embracing mystical pantheism and an authority-centered religious personalism. The conflict between these two approaches may be seen as endemic to the very enterprise of Jewish mysticism. We return to them later, in our discussion of Creation in the Zohar.

The greatest contribution of the Kabbalists, it has been suggested, was the creation of a new religious language against the background of biblical and rabbinic Judaism. The mystics had, and occasionally articulated, a sense that they were reaching beyond philosophy and entering a realm of reality that rational thought was unable to penetrate. The move from rationalist philosophy to mystical ways of thinking (which Rabbi Isaac the Blind described as "sucking" at divine Mind as a child nurses from the breast) was by no means a descent from the intellectual heights to a "lower" state of emotionalism or passion. It was rather an intensification of the contemplative, characterized by what was understood as a breakthrough to a new realm of abstraction or "nothingness." From the Maimonideans, however, the Kabbalists had already obtained a sense of the inadequacy of language to express the content of the contemplative experience. The philosophers' flight from anthropomorphism, carried to the extreme of Maimonides' insistence that descriptions of the divine were possible only in negative terms (the so-called theory of negative attributes), left no reason to hope that still greater depths would be amenable to description by any currently available linguistic tool.

The Kabbalists thus created for themselves a different way of speaking, a language so enriched by networks of symbolic association that their words had about them a new profundity, brought about by those symbolic linkages. For this purpose, the *sefirot* may be viewed not as hypostatic "entities" but as *symbol clusters*, linked by association, the mention or textual occurence of any of which automatically brings to mind all the others as well. For this purpose, the conventional names of the *sefirot* have no particular importance; they are simply one more layer within the complex network of associated symbols.

Let us take an example that will illustrate the point. The third *sefi-rah*, conventionally called *Binah*, is described as the "upper palace," the first home of the divine light. As such it (or "She") is also the higher Tabernacle or the "First Temple." This *sefirah* is also the womb out of which the seven sefirotic "days" are born. She is the one to whom all return and is thus called "primal Mother" (*imma ila'ah*), "penitence" (*teshuvah*), and "jubilee" (*yovel*), as we said earlier. The jubilee association also makes Her "fifty" and links Her with the holiday of *Shavu'ot* (Pentacost) and thus with the revelation of Torah, or the manifestation of the seed of *Ḥokhmah* hidden within Her. But *Binah* also means "understanding," and it is clear that we are speaking about a dintinct aspect of mental activity as well. *Binah* is also the source of language, the quarry out of which the lower *sefirot* and the letters of speech are hewn, the upper Eden out of which the sefirotic "rivers" flow, and the "spring" from which the waters of life are drawn. We could continue to enrich this list by a host of other verbal pictures as well. Joseph Gikatilla's *Sha'arey Orah*, the great symbolary of early Kabbalah, does just that for each of the *sefirot*.

For the Kabbalist, each time any of these words appears in a text—be it the Torah, the prayerbook, or the Talmudic *aggadah*—all the other terms are evoked as well. The same is true, especially in the Zoharic narrative, of seeing or experiencing any of the natural phenomena that are part of such a cluster. To come upon a spring would thus be to think also of *teshuvah*, of the quarry, of the mysterious fifty, and of the source of life. To encounter the word *quarry* in a text—that of *Sefer Yetsirah*, for example—would immediately bring about mental pictures of the Mother, the jubilee, the spring, and all the rest. What then *is* this third *sefirah*, we might ask? True, the Kabbalists did think of it as a hypostasis, as a real if only vaguely accessible "entity" or reality within the Godhead, as a distinct stage in the journey from utter hidden oneness toward self-revelation. But from a functional standpoint, *Binah* is also a cluster of symbols, a nugget of enriched speech, by which the Kabbalist can seek to express something of this deeper-than-accessible reality.

It is no accident that each of these associative clusters contains within it symbols derived from the biblical text and Jewish tradition, personal figures, and representations of the world of nature. In striving for a language that would evoke a response from more profound levels of the human soul, the Kabbalists rediscovered the great power of natural symbols. Including such terms as *sun* and *sky* (*Tif'eret*), *moon*, *sea*, and *earth* (*Malkhut*), *dawn* and *dusk* (*Hesed* and *Gevurah*) in their symbolic repertoire added greatly to the feeling of awe and grandeur evoked by each of the symbolic clusters. Rabbinic Judaism had mostly turned away from the magnificent evocations of God's wonders in Creation so stirringly described by the psalms and prophets. For the rabbis, the greatness of God was primarily to be seen in the profundities of Torah and in its interpretation rather than in the beauties of nature. But the medieval interest in both astronomy and astrology combined with Neoplatonic philosopy to bring forth what has been called a *cosmic spirituality*, one that saw the heavenly spheres as the great testament to God's glory. Kabbalah is part of this phenomenon. It is no accident that the Zohar turns with great frequency and passion to texts from those parts of the Bible that celebrate God's handiwork in Creation. The writings of these ancient poets are fed directly into the network of terms and associations that constitute kabbalistic symbolism.

In addition to the associations found within each symbol cluster, there are groups or patterns of *sefirot* that also give rise to leaps of associative thinking. The connection, for example, of *Hesed-Gevurah-Tif'eret* with the three Biblical patriarchs defines a special sort of link among these three. It then joins them to the opening three blessings of the *amidah* prayer (the central prayer of Jewish worship recited thrice daily), also associated with the patriarchs. Other triads within the tradition then might well be homiletically identified with this fixed group of three. The identification of the four directions with *Hesed-Gevurah-Tif'eret-Malkhut* functions in a similar way, setting the pattern for other fours to be "discovered" as linked to these. The links between the uppermost triad of sefirot and the lower septet, particularly Malkhut, are also of great importance. *Hokhmah* and *Binah* are sometimes depicted as "father" and "mother" to the lower *sefirot*. Sometimes this "parental" link reflects nourishment or source of energy. Both *Yesod* and *Malkhut* are closely related to *Hokhmah* in this way. But in other passages the relationship is more one of structural parallelism. *Binah* is the "upper world" whose likeness is reflected in *Malkhut*, the "lower world" within the sefirotic realm. These two female elements within the Godhead are sometimes depicted as Leah and Rachel, the two wives of Jacob, who stands between them. But elsewhere they are "mother" and "bride" of Jacob-Israel. The male God-figure stands poised between mother and wife, the two females who exercise overwhelming influence over the course of His life, just as do His devotees on earth.

All these patterns of association, and many more, enriched the stock-in-trade available for preachers, helping to join kabbalistic thought and the Jewish homiletical imagination in a link that became increasingly strong over the centuries. They account in large part for the great success of Kabbalah in capturing and maintaining its hold on the religious mentality of Jewry until the dawn of modernity. The complex and highly pictorial forms of symbolic association allowed by the sefirotic system stimulated the creative thinking of many an interpreter and provided a profound linguistic vehicle in which both ideas and experiences could be expressed. Later generations, seeking to expand the "field" of such creativity, tended toward ever-expanding complications of the system. These included the integration of the four "worlds," each of which contained the same tenfold structure, and a sense that each of the *sefirot* contained elements of all the others within it. The symbolic "grid" thus expanded from ten to forty to four hundred. This is not the case, however, in the Zohar, where the richness of fantasy and language themselves are sufficient vehicles for the creative imagination. In fact, it may be said that only the diminishing of that creative spark in later generations forced Kabbalists to rely on the multiplication of categories.

Part II

WHAT IS THE ZOHAR?

4

The Zohar:
Midrash on the Torah

The Zohar, as the contemporary reader of the original encounters it, is
a three-volume work constituting some sixteen-hundred folio pages,
ordered in the form of a commentary on the Torah. The first volume
covers the Zohar on Genesis, the second volume is Zohar on Exodus,
and the third volume comments on the remaining three books of the
Torah. The text is divided into homilies on the weekly Torah portions,
taking the form of an ancient Midrash. Within this form, however, are
included long digressions and subsections of the Zohar that in fact have
no relation to this midrashic structure and seem to be rather arbitrarily
placed in one Torah-portion or another. An addition to the three volumes is *Zohar Ḥadash* ("New Zohar"), a collection of materials that
were omitted from the earliest printed Zohar editions but later culled
from manuscript sources. Here we find addenda to the Torah portions
but also partial commentaries on Ruth, Lamentations, and the Song of
Songs. Another work usually considered part of the Zohar literature
is *Tiqquney Zohar*, a kabbalistic commentary on the opening verse of
Genesis that explicates it in seventy ways. This work, along with the
Ra'aya Meheimna, or "Faithful Shepherd," passages published within the

Zohar itself, mostly taking the form of a commentary on the commandments, is seen by modern scholars to be the work of a slightly
later Kabbalist, one who perhaps worked in the opening decades of the
fourteenth century and saw himself as continuing the Zohar tradition.

The main body of the Zohar takes the form of Midrash: a collection of homiletical explications of the biblical text. The Zohar enters
fully into Midrash as a literary genre, even though that form of writing was considered antiquated in the time and place in which the Zohar was composed. Its authors were especially learned in *aggadah* and
used it ingeniously, often convincingly portraying themselves as ancient midrashic masters, but the anachronism of their style was inten-
tional. The Zohar is an attempt to re-create a form of discourse that
would have seemed appropriate to a work originating in the circle of
its chief speaker, Rabbi Shim'on ben Yoḥai, who lived in the Land of
Israel during the period of the Mishnah, the second century of the
Common Era. In fact, this medieval Midrash is based on a thorough
knowledge of the entire earlier Jewish tradition, including rabbinic,
philosophical, and esoteric works. Its purpose, as quickly becomes clear
to the reader, goes far beyond that of the ancient Midrash. The Zohar
seeks nothing less than to place the kabbalistic tradition, as it had developed over the preceding centuries, into the mouths of these much-
revered sages of antiquity and to use them as its mouthpiece for showing the reader that the entire Torah is alive with kabbalistic secrets and
veiled references to the "mystery of faith" as the Kabbalists taught it. In
this sense the Zohar may be be seen as an attempt to create a new
Midrash or, as one scholar has put it, to bring about a renaissance of
the midrashic art in the Middle Ages.

The homilies of the old Midrash were often preceded by a series of
"openings," proems in which the homilist would demonstrate his skill,
picking his way through a series of biblical associations eventually leading up to the subject at hand. The Zohar too uses such openings, but

with a very different purpose. Here the preacher wants to "open" the scriptural verse itself, remove its outer shell, and find its secret meaning. In this way the verse itself may serve as an opening or gateway into the "upper" world for the one who reads it. This leads us closer to the real purpose of Zoharic exegesis. The Zohar wants to take the reader inside the divine life. It wants ever to retell the story of the flow of the *sefirot*, their longings and union, the arousal of love above, and the way in which that arousal causes blessing to flow throughout the worlds. This is the essential story of Kabbalah, and the Zohar finds it in verse after verse, portion after portion, of the Torah text. But each retelling offers a new and often startlingly different perspective on this essential truth. The Zohar is ever enriching the kabbalistic narrative by means of retelling it from the vantage point of still another hermeneutic insight. On each page another verse, word, or tale of the Torah is opened or "uncovered" to reveal new insight into the great story of the Zohar, that which it proffers as the truth of the Torah, of the cosmos, and of the reader's soul.

In the series of homilies by various speakers on a particular verse or moment in the scriptural text, the Zohar takes its readers through multiple layers of understanding, reaching from the surface level of "plain" meaning into ever more profound revelations. A great love of language is revealed in this process; plays on words and subtle reshadings of meaning often serve as pathways leading toward a total reconfiguration of the Scripture at hand. For this reason, the Zohar's best readers, both traditional and modern, are those who share its endless fascination with the mystery of words and letters, including both their aural and their graphic (or "spoken" and "written") manifestations.

Other Kabbalists contemporaneous with the Zohar offered multi-leveled readings of Scripture as well. Rabbi Bahya ben Asher of Barcelona immediately comes to mind. His Torah commentary, written in the 1290s, offers the clearest example of the fourfold interpretation of

Scripture in its Jewish form: verse after verse is read first for its plain meaning, then according to "the way of Midrash," "the way of intellect" or philosophical allegory, and "the way of Kabbalah." Rabbi Bahya's work is in fact important as one of the earliest sources for quotations from the Zohar.

The Zohar offers no such neat classifications. Insights suggested by a group of "companions" discussing a text may bounce back and forth from readings that could be (and sometimes indeed are) found in earlier midrashic works to ways of reading that belong wholly to the world of Kabbalah. Kabbalistic interpretations are sometimes so well "sewn" into the fabric of midrashic readings that the reader is left wondering whether the kabbalistic referent might not indeed be the "real" meaning of a given biblical verse or rabbinic passage. In one well-known text,[1] the Zohar refers to mystical interpretations as the "soul" of Torah, distinguished from the narrative that forms the outward "garments" and from the legal derivations that serve as Torah's "body" (playing on the phrase *gufei Torah*, "bodies of Torah," that in rabbinic parlance means "essential teachings"). That text also suggests a further level of readings, the "innermost soul" of Torah, that will not be fully revealed until messianic times. But when encountering actual passages from the Zohar, it is not easy to determine just where one stands in the process of undressing the textual bride. Here as almost everywhere, the poesis of the Zohar overflows the banks, thwarting any attempt at gradation or definition. It is mostly within the area of "soul" or kabbalistic readings that the assembled sages reveal layer after layer, showing that this level of reading itself contains inexhaustible riches of the imagination. There is not a single mystical interpretation of a verse or passage that is the secret in the eyes of the Zohar. "Secret" (*sod* in Hebrew, *raza* in Aramaic) is rather a method, a way of reading that contains endless individual secrets within it.

1. 3:152a.

The language of sefirotic symbolism offers the Zohar limitless op-
portunies for creative interpretations of Scripture. On the one hand, the
Zohar's speakers and authors exult in the newness and originality of this
exegesis. Rabbi Shim'on and his disciples speak glowingly of *ḥiddushei
Torah*, new interpretations of Torah, and their great value. God and the
angels join in rejoicing over each new insight. On the other hand, the
Zohar also seeks to deny the newness of kabbalistic interpretation. Not
only is the work itself allegedly an ancient one, but the interpretive craft
of the Zohar also goes to a higher, deeper, and hence more "ancient"
level of the text. As the highest rung within the Godhead is sometimes
called *Attiqa*, the elder or "ancient one," so does profound interpretation
take Torah "back to its antiquity," to its original, pristine, highest state.

The Zohar stands within the long tradition of Jewish devotion to
sacred study as a religious act. The faithful are commanded to "contemplate it day and night" (Josh. 1:8), which is traditionally taken to
mean that the study and elaboration of Torah are ideally the full-time
obligation of the entire community of male Israelites (women were ex-
empted from the obligation to study and only rarely were they offered
more than a rudimentary education). This community viewed the
Torah as an object of love, and an eros of Torah study is depicted in
many passages in the rabbinic *aggadah*. Based on biblical images of feminine wisdom, Torah was described as the daughter and delight of God
and as Israel's bride. The study of Torah, especially the elaboration of its
law, was described by the sages as courtship and sometimes even as the
shy, scholarly bridegroom's act of love, the consummation of his sacred
marriage. The Midrash on the Song of Songs, compiled in the seventh
or eighth century, devotes a large part of its exegesis of that erotic text
to discussing the revelation at Sinai and the delights of both God and
the sages in the study of Torah.

The Zohar is well aware of these precedents and expands on them
in its own richer and even more daring version of *amor dei intellectualis*.

The lush and well-watered gardens of the Song of Songs are the constant dwelling-place of the Zohar, where frequent invocation of the Canticle is the order of the day. In the Kabbalists' literary imagination, the gardens of eros in the Song of Songs, the *pardes* or "orchard" of mystical speculation itself, and the mystical Garden of Eden, into which God wanders each night "to take delight in the souls of the righteous," have been thoroughly linked with one another. Genesis' description of Paradise—"a river goes forth from Eden to water the garden, whence it divides into four streams" (2:10)—and certain key verses of the Canticle—"a spring amid the gardens, a well of living waters, flowing from Lebanon" (4:15) and others—are quoted endlessly to invoke the sense that to dwell in mystical exegesis is to sit in the shade of God's garden. Even more: the mystical exegete comes to understand that all of these gardens are but reflections of the true inner divine garden, the world of the sefirot, which Sefer ha-Bahir had already described as lush with trees, springs, and ponds of water.

The Zohar is devoted to the full range of religious obligations that the Torah places on the community of Israel. The mysteries of the commandments and the rhythms of the sacred year very much occupy its pages, even if we discount the somewhat later *Ra'aya Meheimna* ("Faithful Shepherd") section, which is almost wholly devoted to this subject. Both prayer and the ancient Temple ritual, the classic Jewish forms of devotion, are given lofty kabbalistic interpretations, and the figure of the priest in particular is central to the Zoharic imagination, as we shall see later. Still, it is fair to say that the central religious act for the Zohar is the very one in which its heroes are engaged, as described throughout its pages, and that is the act of study and interpretation of Torah. Again and again Rabbi Shim'on waxes eloquent in praise of those who study Torah, especially those who do so after midnight. They indeed take the place of the priests and Levites of old, "who stand in the house of the Lord by night" (Ps. 134:1). Those who

awaken nightly to study the secrets of Torah become the earthly attendants of the divine bride, ushering her into the chamber where she
will unite at dawn with her heavenly spouse. This somewhat modest
depiction of the mystic devotee's role in the *hieros gamos*, or sacred marriage rite, that stands at the center of the kabbalistic imagination does
not exclude a level of emotional-mystical reality in which the Kabbalist himself is also the lover of that bride and a full participant in,
rather than merely an attendant to, the act of union.

> Torah in the Zohar is not conceived as a text, as an object, or as mate-
> rial, but as a living divine presence, engaged in a mutual relationship
> with the person who studies her. More than that, in the Zoharic con-
> sciousness Torah is compared to a beloved who carries on with her lov-
> ers a mutual and dynamic courtship. The Zohar on the portion *Mishpa-
> tim* contains, within the literary unit known as *Sava de-Mishpatim*, a
> description of a maiden in a palace. Here the way of the Torah's lover is
> compared to the way of a man with a maid. Arousal within Torah is like
> an endless courting of the beloved: constant walking about the gates of
> her palace, an increasing passion to read her letters, the desire to see the
> beloved's face, to reveal her, and to be joined with her. The beloved in
> the nexus of this relationship is entirely active. She sends signals of her
> interest to her lover, she intensifies his passionate desire for her by games
> of revealing and hiding. She discloses secrets that stir his curiosity. She
> desires to be loved. The beloved is disclosed in an erotic progression be-
> fore her lover out of a desire to reveal secrets that have been forever hid-
> den within her. The relationship between Torah and her lover, like that
> of man and maiden in this parable, is dynamic, romantic, and erotic. This
> interpretive axiom of the work, according to which the relationship be-
> tween student and that studied is not one of subject and object but of
> subject and subject, even an erotic relationship of lover and beloved,
> opens a great number of new possibilities. . . . [2]

Seeing the act of Torah study as the most highly praised form of devotional activity places the Zohar squarely within the Talmudic tradi-

2. Melila Hellner-Eshed, "The Language of Mystical Experience in the Zohar: The
Zohar Through Its Own Eyes." (Doctoral dissertation, Hebrew University, 2000), p. 19.

tion and at the same time provides a setting in which to go far beyond it. Here, unlike in the rabbinic sources, the *content* of the exegesis as well as the *process* is erotic in character. The Talmudic Rabbi Akiva, the chief hero of the rabbinic romance with the text, was inspired by his great love of Torah to derive "heaps and heaps of laws from the crowns on each of the letters." It was the early rabbis' intense devotion to the text and to the *process* of Torah study that was so aptly described by the erotic metaphor. But the laws derived in the course of this passionate immersion in the text might deal with heave offerings and tithes or ritual defilement and ablutions; all of these were equally to be celebrated as resulting from the embrace of Torah. That indeed is the genius of Rabbi Akiva's school of thought: *all* of Torah, even the seemingly most mundane, belongs to the great mystical moment of Sinai, the day when God gave Torah to Israel and proclaimed His love for her in the Song of Songs. But the authors of the Zohar crave more than this. The *content* as well as the *process* has to reveal the great secret of unity, not just the small secrets of one law or another. In the Zohar the true subject matter that the Kabbalist finds in every verse is the *hieros gamos* itself, the mystical-erotic union of the divine male and female, the eros that underlies and transforms Torah, making it into a symbolic textbook on the inner life of God.

5

The Zohar Narrative

The Zohar is not only a book of Torah interpretation. It is also very much the story of a particular group of students of the Torah, a peripatetic band of disciples gathered around their master, Rabbi Shim'on ben Yoḥai. In the main body of the Zohar there appear eight such disciples: Rabbi El'azar (the son of Rabbi Shim'on), Rabbi Abba, Rabbi Yehudah, Rabbi Yitsḥak, Rabbi Ḥizkiyah, Rabbi Ḥiyya, Rabbi Yose, and Rabbi Yeisa. A significant part of the Zohar text is devoted to tales of their wanderings and adventures, proclamations of their great love for one another, accounts of their devotion to their master, and echoes of the great pleasure he takes in hearing their teachings. In these tales, while on the road, wandering from place to place in the Holy Land, they encounter various other teachers, in the form of mysterious elders, wondrous children, merchants, and donkey drivers, all of whom possess of secrets that they share with this band of loving and faithful companions. Usually these mysterious teachers know more than the wanderers expect, and Rabbi Shim'on's disciples are often outshone in wisdom by these most unlikely figures. That too is part of the Zohar's story. A contemporary scholar notes that more than three hundred whole and partial stories of this sort are contained within the Zohar text. In some places the narrative shifts from the earthly setting to one that is partly in heaven or in "the Garden of Eden," in which the master is replaced by God Himself, who proclaims His pleasure at the innovations offered as the Kabbalists engage in Torah.

These tales of Rabbi Shim'on and his disciples wandering about the Galilee a thousand years before the Zohar was written are clearly works of fiction. But to say so is by no means to deny the possibility that a very real mystical brotherhood underlies the Zohar and shapes its spiritual character. Anyone who reads the Zohar over an extended period will come to see that the interface among the companions and the close relationship between the tales of their wanderings and the homilies those wanderings occasion are not the result of fictional imagination alone. Whoever wrote the work knew very well how fellow students respond to companionship and support and are inspired by one another's glowing renditions of a text. He (or they) has felt the warm glow of a master's praise and the shame of being shown up by a stranger in the face of one's peers. Leaving aside for now the question of who actually penned the words, we can say that the Zohar *reflects the experience* of a kabbalistic circle. It is one of a series of such circles of Jewish mystics, stretching back in time to Qumran, Jerusalem, Provence, and Gerona, and forward in history to Safed, Padua, Miedzybozh, Bratslav, and again to Jerusalem. A small circle of initiates gathered about a master is the way Kabbalah has always happened, and the Zohar is no exception. In fact, the collective experience of this group around Rabbi Shim'on ben Yoḥai as "recorded" in the Zohar forms the paradigm for all later Jewish mystical circles.

The group life reflected in the text is that of a band of living Kabbalists, except that they occupied Castile of the thirteenth century rather than Erets Israel of the second. They lived in Toledo and Guadalajara rather than Tiberias and Sepphoris. Whether these real Kabbal-

ists wandered about in the Spanish countryside as their fictional counterparts did in the Holy Land is hard to know, but they certainly felt
that the most proper setting for study of Torah was outdoors, especially
in a garden or a grove of trees. Occasionally the companions in the Zohar's pages have conversations indoors, as when the disciples visit Rabbi
Shim'on or travel to the home of Rabbi Pinhas ben Ya'ir. Interestingly,
no house of study or synagogue appears as a setting for any of their encounters. The Zohar very much prefers that they take place under the
shade of a certain tree, at a spring of water, or at some similar place that
might call to mind a verse from a psalm or the Song of Songs, with
which a homily might then open.

The frequent references in the text to the importance of secret
Torah study at night raises the likelihood that this group of Spanish
Kabbalists shared for some time, as a regular, ritualized activity, a late-
night session for the study of Kabbalah. If they were anything like
their fictional counterparts, these sessions began after midnight and
went until dawn, concluding with morning prayers. These nightly
gatherings (of course there is no way to be certain whether or for
how long they did actually take place) were omitted on the Sabbath,
when it was the companion's duty to be at home with his wife. They
reached their annual climax on the eve of Shavu'ot, when the vigil
was in preparation for a new receiving of the Torah. The intense climax of the Zohar narrative is the tale of two great and highly ritualized meetings of master and disciples in the *Idra*, a special chamber of
assembly (see further discussion of the *Idrot* in Chapter Fifteen). In the
first of these two assemblies, three of the companions die in the ecstacy of their mystical devotions. The story of the second meeting, the
Idra Zuta or Lesser Assembly, records the death of Rabbi Shim'on himself and forms the grand conclusion of the Zohar.

Gershom Scholem once suggested that the Zohar takes the form of
a "mystical novel." This suggestion is particularly intriguing because the

Zohar appeared in Spain some three hundred years before Cervantes, who is often seen as the father of the modern novel. One may see the tales of Rabbi Shim'on and his companions as a sort of novel in formation, but it is clear that the form is quite rudimentary. When the Zohar wants to express an idea, it needs to slip back into the more familiar literary form of textual hermeneutics. The novelist in the classic post-Cervantes sense is one who can develop ideas or suggest complex thought patterns by means of character development and plot, rather than by having the characters assemble and make a series of speeches to one another (though such moments are not entirely unknown in later fiction). It might be interesting to place the Zohar into the setting of such works as medieval troubador romances, Chaucer's fourteenth-century *Canterbury Tales*, or the *Thousand and One Nights*. All of these are narrative cycles, frameworks of story into which smaller units (in these cases narrative, in the Zohar's case homiletical) can be fitted. All of them, too, may be seen as precursors of the novel.

The peregrinations of Rabbi Shim'on and his disciples are more, however, than the "story" of the Zohar, whether fictional or masking a historical reality. In the Zohar everything is indeed more than it appears to be. Master and disciples represent wandering Israel, both the ancient tribes in the wilderness, on their way to the promised land, and the people of Israel in their present exile. While the ancient rabbis suggest to the would-be scholar to "exile yourself to a place of Torah,"[1] for the Zohar exile or wandering is itself that place. The "place of Torah" is indeed wherever the companions happen to be, the home of the master or the grove of trees. In words that they might prefer, it can be said that the "garden" of mystical conversation follows them wherever they wander, just as Miriam's movable well gave drink to Israel throughout their forty-year trek through the wilderness. The adventures of the companions show their participation in Israel's greatest suffering, that of exile.

1. Mishnah Avot 4:14.

Israel's historic exile, however, is itself symbolic, an earthly representation of a still greater exile, that of the *Shekhinah* from her divine
spouse. The nature and origin of this inner divine "exile" together
constitute one of the Kabbalists' great mysteries. Some passages, both
in the Zohar and in earlier sources, attribute this exile to the sin of
Adam and Eve. In this sense Kabbalah may be said to have a true sense
of the "fall" or "original sin" of humans, much more so than the older
rabbinic sources. The world as first created was a true Garden of Eden
because the blessed Holy One and *Shekhinah* were "face to face,"
joined in constant embrace like that of *Ḥokhmah* and *Binah*. Divine
blessing thus coursed through the system without interruption, flowing through all of *Shekhinah*'s "hosts" and "palaces" into an idealized
lower world as well. Only Adam and Eve's sin, sometimes depicted as
that of separating *Shekhinah* from the upper *sefirot* to worship her
alone (symbolized by the separation of the Tree of Knowledge from
its roots in the Tree of Life), disturbed this initial harmony. Since the
expulsion from Eden, the union of *Tif'eret* and *Malkhut*, or Blessed
Holy One and *Shekhinah*, has been sporadic rather than constant, dependent upon the balance of human virtue and transgression.

Other passages, however, express a somewhat darker vision of the
exile within God. They claim that the very existence of the lower
worlds is an after-effect of divine exile and would not have taken place
without it. Some of these sources employ the old Platonic myth of an-
drogyny, embedded in a midrashic description of Adam and Eve, to explain the cosmic reality. Adam and Eve, according to the *aggadah*,[2] were
Siamese twins, conjoined back to back. This single being is that described in Genesis 1:29: "God created the human in His form; in the
divine form He created him, male and female He made them." The
forming of Eve from Adam's rib (or "side") in the next chapter was the
separation of this pair, in which they were first turned face-to-face, to-

2. Babylonian Talmud Berakhot 61a.

ward one another, so that they might meet, see one another, and unite to propagate the species, fulfilling God's first command. The Kabbalists claim that in this sense, too, humans are made in God's image: *Tif'eret* and *Malkhut*, back to back, were a single entity. They had to be "sawed" apart (a rather violent choice of verb) so that they might be properly united. Only through this union did the divine life begin to flow outward, giving life to worlds below. In order for our life to come about, in other words, God had to undergo a transformative act of great pain, one in which the divine became separated from itself, its future reunification depending entirely upon the actions of these creatures below. According to this story, exile and suffering are inherent in the cosmos, and the balm provided by human goodness is somewhat superficial, an oasis of relief in the wandering that is indeed the necessary human and cosmic condition.

It is this exile that the Kabbalists were acting out in their wanderings through the Galilee of their imagination. In this sense it may indeed be said that the Zohar in its entirety is a symbolic work rather than a collection of symbolic interpretations of Scripture. The narratives themselves may be seen as the most profoundly symbolic and kabbalistic part of the Zohar's *oeuvre*, not just a framework into which the homilies are woven. The tales of these wandering holy men, seeking to live fully in God's image through the act of studying and expounding upon God's Torah, is the tale of God's own exile, inherent in the divine choice to come forth and be revealed in this lowly, corporeal world.

6

Mysticism of the Zohar

Our discussion leads us now to confront directly the question of the Zohar and religious-mystical experience. A first reading of the Zohar might give one the impression that it is more *mythical* than *mystical* in content, that it is more a narrative of cosmic origins and structures than of inner experience, the soul, or higher states of consciousness. But this view is partially misleading. To read the Zohar well is to fathom the experiential dimension of the entire text, including narrative, exegesis, cosmology, and all the rest. The Kabbalist speaking in the sefirotic idiom is laying bare the innermost structure of reality as he both understands and *experiences* it. That same structure is reflected in the cosmos, in Torah, and in the human (or more precisely, "Jewish") soul. The language of sefirotic symbolism provides a new lens through which to see all of Torah. But the power of that reading, especially as practiced in the circle of the Zohar, offers more than a hermeneutic. To open one's inner eye to the new reality created by that pattern of thinking is to live within the realm of the *sefirot* themselves. The transformations of language and inner experience go hand in hand with one another; the breakthrough in consciousness to a higher realm of contemplative existence is conveyed through the vehicle of self-expression in sefirotic terms. Therefore, to speak of the origins of the sefirotic universe, or to interpret the Torah text in terms of sefirotic symbols, is also to enter into those places within the soul. For the speakers within the Zohar, as for the ideal Kabbalist in any time, to speak of the *sefirot* is not simply to draw on a body of esoteric knowledge, but rather to enter the inner universe where sefirotic language is the guide to measured experience.

The authors of the Zohar did not generally feel the need to tell their readers that this is the case. In a work written for initiates, the link between the intellectual and experiential dimensions was taken for granted. It is primarily the frequent expressions of enthusiasm and ecstacy with which the text is dotted that serve to indicate how deeply and personally the sefirotic teachings were felt. The repeated refrain "Had I come into the world only to hear this, it would be sufficient!" and the kisses showered upon speakers by their grateful companions make it clear to any but the most obtuse of readers that in the pages of the Zohar we are witnessing both the ecstatic heights and the contemplative depths that constitute the shared inner life of a vital mystical circle, not merely a series of exercises in biblical homiletics interspersed with exotic stories.

The sefirotic universe as a representation of inner religious experience may be described in more specific ways as well, though these are surely not exhaustive. The "descent" of the *sefirot*, beginning with *Keter*, is said to describe the emergence of God from hiddenness to revelation. Both the creation of the world and the giving of Torah are this-worldly extensions of that inner divine process. On a more realistic plane, however, so too is the mystic's own inner life. Sefirotic symbolism provides a language for describing the mystic's own return from an experience of absorption in the "Nothingness" of God and gradual reintegration into the framework of full human personality, the reemergence of conscious selfhood. It should be emphasized that the Zohar never makes such a claim. In general the Kabbalists were loath to speak too openly about the experiential aspects of their teaching. Especially when it came to the highest triad of the sefirotic world, to speak in terms that claimed direct experience was considered far beyond the bounds of propriety. But one who reads the Kabbalists with an eye to comparative and phenomenological descriptions of mysticism cannot but suspect that such experience is the source of these descriptions. The accounts of a mysterious energy that flows from undefined endlessness, through a primal arousal of will, into a single point that is the start of all being, and thence into the womb-palace, where the self (divine or human) is born, sound like descriptions found elsewhere in mystical literature of the rebirth of personality that follows the contemplative experience. Even though the Zohar depicts it chiefly as the original journey of God, we understand that the mystical life repeats that divine process. In fact, it is out of their own experience that mystics know what they do of the original journey on which theirs is patterned. Perhaps one can go even a step farther to claim that the constant movement within the sefirotic world, including both the flow of energy "downward" from *Keter* and the rising up of *Malkhut* and the lower worlds into the divine heights, represents the dynamic inner life of the mystic and the spiritual motion that ever animates his soul. It is these nuances of inner movement that constitute the "real" subject of a very large part of the Zohar and the world it creates. To most fully appreciate the Zohar as a mystical text is to understand these movements as reverberations in the mystic's soul of events as they transpire within the divine reality, and *vice versa*.

When the Zohar does speak of mystical experience, it is largely through use of the term *devequt*, "attachment" or "cleaving" to God, and its Aramaic cognates. Ever since the early rabbinic discussions of

Deuteronomy 4:4 ("You who cleave to YHVH your God are all alive today") and 10:20 ("Fear YHVH your God, cleave to Him and serve Him"), *devequt* has played a central role in the devotional life of pious Jews. But the Zohar is also quick to associate this term with its first biblical usage in Genesis 2:24, where man "cleaves to his wife and they become one flesh." Attachment to God, for the Zohar, is erotic attachment, whether referring to the Kabbalist's own attachment to God by means of Torah, to *Shekhinah*'s link to the upper "male" *sefirot* as God's bride, or in the rare passages where Moses becomes the kabbalistic hero and himself weds *Shekhinah*, entering the Godhead in the male role. The contemplative and erotic aspects of attachment to God are just different ways of depicting the same reality, quite wholly inseparable from one another.

With the experience of human love and sexuality as its chief metaphor for intimacy, the Zohar depicts *devequt* as a temporary and fleeting experience. Scholars have debated for some time the question of whether true *unio mystica* is to be found in the Zohar. But this debate may itself hinge on the sexual analogy. Is true loss of self or absorption within the union to be attained in sexual climax? How does one begin to answer such a question without interviewing all of the world's great lovers? Whether or not the experience underlying countless passages in the Zohar can be described as "union" lies, I would submit, beyond our ken. But it is clear that no possibility of *permanent* bliss is offered to those still attached to bodily existence; only in the world to come will the disembodied spirits of the righteous enjoy the endless delight of basking in the divine presence. Religious experience in this world is but a foretaste of that eternal joy.

The attachment to the erotic metaphor colors the Zohar's description of religious experience in other ways as well. Throughout the book there is a fascination with the reproductive process, including sexual arousal, courtship, union, birth, and nursing, that can be characterized as childlike or perhaps Edenic.[1] The union of male and female *is* the great cosmic mystery, one in which the Kabbalist himself is engaged as he speaks, through the act of studying and teaching Torah. This means that verbal and physical creativity, or what we would call the *creative* and the *procreative* processes, are inseparable from one another. The ancient analogy made in *Sefer Yetsirah* between *berit ha-lashon* and *berit ha-ma'or*, the verbal and the sexual covenants, inspires the Kabbalist to an understanding that the creative expression coming forth from these two unique and parallel organs, mouth and genitalia, both located in the middle of the human body, represents a single and sublime mystery.

As the Zohar seeks to develop a language for what we may call its *eros* of poetic creativity, exegesis of the Song of Songs plays a major role. The Zohar turns with great frequency, especially in its proems, or homiletical "warm-ups," to that great font of sacred *eros*. The Song of Songs, a text in which *eros* in fact remains unconsumated, offers poetic language for every other aspect of the complete drama of courting, including even loss, separation, and longing. All of these elements come to the fore in the Zohar's frequent disquisitions on the Song, which is often surprisingly linked to verses describing some aspect of the Tabernacle cult or another seemingly dry detail of biblical law. These texts are utterly transformed by association with the Canticle. The Torah text as a whole, it may be said, is "washed over" in an eroticizing bath created by repeated juxtaposition of Torah texts with verses of the Song of Songs, poetically enriching the *eros* of sefirotic symbolisation itself. The historical context for this inner divine reading of the Song of Songs is discussed in the next chapter.

The writers of the Zohar learned from the Neoplatonist milieu within which they lived to speak of the flow of energy, usually de-

---

1. The formal schematization of these developmental stages within each element of the God was to have an important role in the later Lurianic Kabbalah.

scribed as light, from one cosmic realm to the next. The Neoplatonists tended to emphasize the diminution of that light as it reached "downward" toward the material plane. For the Kabbalist, this constantly renewed pouring forth of divine presence could be felt both in the daily renewal of nature and in the creative vigor of Torah interpretation. He sought to align himself with the cosmic flow, in order to receive its bounty, but also to act in such ways as to stimulate the flow itself. Images of both light and water abound in the Zohar's pages to describe the *shefa*, the endless flux of divine bounty that sustains the universe. In the context of our earlier discussion, it is clear that this fluid is also the divine seed, that which enters into *Shekhinah* and allows for the constant rebirth of life in the realms beneath her.

Read this way, the Zohar is very much a mystical, often even an ecstatic, work, or at least one in which the ecstatic dimension is highly developed. One of the strongest expressions of this reality is found in the Zohar's powerful and poetic soliloquies on the word *zohar* itself, and on the verse (Daniel 12:3) from which the work's title is taken: "The enlightened shall shine like the radiance [*zohar*] of the sky, and those who lead multitudes to righteousness, like the stars, forever." *Zohar* represents a hidden radiance issuing forth from the highest sefirotic realms, a showering of sparks lighting up all that comes into its path. Its inspiration is surely the night sky, the wondrous event of shooting stars against the background of the Milky Way. But like all such images in mystical literature, the beacon of light or drop of divine seed is a pictorial representation of an event that takes place also within the mystic's heart, the inspiration that "sparks" this creative vision.

The inner event of this radiant presence is outwardly manifest in the shining gaze of the Kabbalist's face. "The enlightened shall shine" is also understood in this rather literal way. Here, as frequently in the Zohar, there is an assimilation of the Kabbalist into the biblical description of Moses as he emerged from the Tent of Meeting, his face glowing with the radiant presence of God. But the Kabbalist is also Moses' brother Aaron, the ancient priest whose face shines with divine presence as he bestows the blessing of God's own countenance upon the children of Israel. "May the Lord cause His face to shine upon you" (Num. 6:25) is seen as the Torah's personified way of calling forth the same light that the Kabbalist as Neoplatonist perceives to be shining forth from one cosmic rung to another. He now seeks to become the earthly bearer of that light, transmitting it to his community of disciples and readers. This is the Kabbalist (most often personified in the Zohar by Rabbi Shim'on ben Yohai) in the role of *tsaddiq*, righteous conveyer of divine light.

A main purpose of the Zohar is to arouse within the reader a constant longing for such "enlightenment" or inspiration. The great religious creativity—and even the ecstatic deaths—of Rabbi Shim'on and his disciples are meant to induce in the reader a sense that he too, as an initiate into the Zohar's secrets, may continue in this path. While no generation before the advent of messiah will fully equal that of Rabbi Shim'on, all those who come in his wake are encouraged to follow in his path. The Zohar is thus a highly evocative work, one that seeks to create and sustain a mood of ecstatic devotion. Certain familiar biblical verses, including the "garden" passages mentioned earlier, are used as awakeners—one might almost think of them as "bells"—to regularly restimulate awareness, rousing the reader from his daily torpor and reminding him of the constant vital flow needed to quicken the cosmos. This reminder is meant to renew and refresh his participation in Israel's great collective task of rousing *Shekhinah*. She in turn awakens her divine Lover to release the flow of light-water-seed, enveloping her in his presence and renewing the universal flow of life.

The "Eden" (or "Lebanon") whence that flow is to come is an accessible if hidden rung within the divine and human self. It is not just an ancient and lost site of the biblical tale, nor is it only the "paradise" to which souls will ascend after death. Eden is the "upper world," a recondite and inward aspect of being that is mirrored in the "garden," the One who needs to be watered by that flow. We creatures of the "lower world," souls who are the fruit of trees growing in the garden, need to trace back the course of that river to its source, linking the upper and lower worlds (*Binah* and *Shekhinah*, but also *Shekhinah* and "this" world, or *Shekhinah* and the soul) so that the flow will never cease.

Reflecting on these nature-evoking verses takes us back to the typically outdoor settings of the companions' conversations, mentioned earlier. These settings represent the varied topography of the Land of Israel as it existed in the authors' imagination, including deserts and vast, forboding mountains as well as fertile oases and springs of water. The lush garden, especially as evoked in the Song of Songs, is a particularly characteristic setting to inspire such conversations. It may be connected to the much older designation of the "place" of mystical speculation as *pardes* or "orchard." But it is also related to the verses quoted in this chapter and to the series of connected gardens in which the Kabbalist sees himself as dwelling. This world is a lower garden, needing constantly to be watered by sources from above, ultimately by the love and sustenance that is the gift of *Shekhinah*. But she too is a garden, nurtured by the river that comes forth from the hidden Eden, itself also a "garden" in some unknown, mysterious way. Somewhere between this world and *Shekhinah* stands the "Garden of Eden" that contains the souls of the righteous, both those who have completed their time on earth and those not yet born. It too is divided into "upper" and "lower" sections, described in various mythical ways.

All of these gardens are linked to one another. The Kabbalist sitting and studying Torah with his companions in an earthly garden—physically in Castile but imaginatively in the Holy Land—is aware that at the same moment the righteous in the Garden of Eden are also engaged in such study. Their garden is open from above, because it is taught that God Himself descends into that Garden to take delight in the souls of the righteous.[2] All of these point still higher, toward the sefirotic gardens, and all these levels of the imagination fructify and enrich one another. The sweet aromas rising from these gardens also play a role in the descriptions of mystical intoxication frequently found in the Zohar's pages.

2. Gardens were an important feature of upper-class life in both Muslim and Christian Spain; it was through medieval Spain that gardening entered Europe. See D. Fairchild Ruggles, *Garden, Landscape, and Vision in the Palaces of Islamic Spain* (University Park: Pennsylvania State University Press, 2000), especially "The Garden as Paradise on Earth," pp. 215–20.

7

The Zohar
in Historical Context

We have spoken of the emergence of Kabbalah into public discourse as a result of the ongoing struggle with philosophy that characterized Provencal and Catalonian Jewry in the century after Maimonides. The Zohar, emerging in the last decades of the thirteenth century, contained strong echoes of that conflict, even though its sharpest phase had by then passed into history. There happens to have survived a copy of Maimonides' *Guide for the Perplexed* that was written for Rabbi Moses de Leon, the central figure of the circle in which the Zohar was composed. That manuscript stands alongside many references in the Zohar text itself, as well as in de Leon's Hebrew treatises, telling us that the greatest work of Kabbalah was written partly in self-conscious response to what was universally taken to be the greatest work of Jewish philosophy.

The Zohar also has to be seen, however, in the broader context in which it was written. I refer to the life of Spanish Jewry during the years of the Reconquista, in which small, threatened Jewish communities lived in the context of a proud, fervent, and militant Christianity. While the closing decades of the thirteenth century were not a particularly terrible period in the long history of Jewish-Catholic relations in Spain—certainly nothing to compare with what was to come a century later—Jews did live with a constant sense of being surrounded and besieged by Christian triumphalism. The Zohar was composed in Castile of the late thirteenth century, a period that marked the near-completion of the Reconquista and something of a golden age of enlightenment in the history of medieval Christian Spain. As the wars of conquest ended, the monarchy was able to ground itself and establish central authority over the semi-independent and often unruly Spanish nobility. This included responsibility for protection of the Jews, who generally fared better at the hands of kings than at the arbitrary mercy of local rivals. Alfonso X (1252–1284) was known as *el Sabio* or "the Wise" because of his interest in the sciences, which he was willing to learn from Jews and Muslims when necessary, as well as in history, literature, and art.

Jews retained a high degree of juridical and cultural autonomy, as well as freedom of religious practice, in Castile of this period. They constituted a significant percentage of city and town dwellers, generally choosing to live in self-enclosed neighborhoods and communities. But Jews were seen by Christian society as barely tolerated outsiders, and they viewed themselves as humiliated and victimized exiles. As an emerging class of Christian burghers came to see the Jews as rivals, the economic opportunities afforded by the early Reconquista years were gradually eroded. Jews were required to wear distinguishing garb, synagogue building was restricted, and various burdens of extra taxation came to be an expected part of Jewish life.

Most significantly, Jews were under constant pressure to convert to Christianity in the atmosphere of a church triumphant with the glory of having vanquished the Moorish armies and standing on the verge of ending the "stain" of Islamic incursion into Christian Europe. Alfonso X commissioned translations of both the Qur'an and the Talmud into Castilian, partly out of scholarly interest but also as an aid to the ongoing missionary campaign. The success of the Reconquista itself was trumpeted as great testimony to the validity of Christian claims. The Christian supersessionist theology of the age claimed tirelessly that Judaism after Christ was an empty shell, a formalist attachment to the past, lacking in true faith. This message was delivered regularly in polemical writings, in sermons that Jews were forced to hear, and in casual encounters between Jews and Christians. We should remember that Jews in Spain spoke the same language as their neighbors and lived with them in the towns and cities. Their degree of linguistic and cultural alienation from their surroundings was significantly less than that of later Jews in Eastern Europe, the lens through which all Jewish diaspora experience is often mistakenly viewed in our time.

In this context, the Zohar may be viewed as a grand defense of Judaism, a poetic demonstration of the truth and superiority of Jewish faith. Its authors knew a great deal about Christianity, mostly from observing it at close hand but also from reading certain Christian works, including the New Testament, which Dominicans and other eager seekers of converts were only too happy to place in the hands of literate and inquisitive Jews. The Kabbalists' attitude toward the religion of their Christian neighbors was a complex one, and it has come down to us through a veil of self-censorship. Jews writing in medieval Europe, especially those promulgating innovative religious teachings that were controversial even within the Jewish community, must have been well aware that their works would be read by Christian censors (often themselves Jewish apostates) who would make them pay dearly for outright insults to the Christian faith.

The Zohar is filled with disdain and sometimes even outright hatred for the Gentile world. Continuing in the old midrashic tradition of repainting the subtle shadings of biblical narrative in moralistic black and white, the Zohar pours endless heaps of wrath and malediction on Israel's enemies. In the context of biblical commentary, these are always such ancient figures as Esau, Pharaoh, Amalek, Balaam, and the mixed multitude of runaway slaves who left Egypt with Israel, a group treated by the Zohar with special venom. All of these were rather safe objects for attack, but it does not take much imagination to realize that the true addressee of this resentment was the oppressor in whose midst the authors lived. This becomes significantly clearer when we consider the Zohar's comments on the religion of these ancient enemies. It castigates them repeatedly as worshipers of the demonic and practitioners of black magic, as enemies of divine unity and therefore dangerous disturbers of the cosmic balance by which the world survives. Israel, and especially the kabbalistic "companions" who understood this situation, are told to do all they can to right the balance and save the *Shekhinah* from those dark forces and their vast network of accursed supporters on earth. As Moses fought off the evil spells of Balaam, darkest of all magicians, in his day, so must the disciples of Rabbi Shim'on fight those evil forces that stand opposed to the dawning of the messianic light that is soon to come.

All of this is said, of course, without a single negative word about Christianity. But Rabbi Shim'on and his second-century companions lived in a time when the enemies of biblical Israel had long ago disappeared from the earth. They had been replaced by the Roman Empire —pagan in the days of Rabbi Shim'on, to be sure, but by the Zohar's time, long associated with Christendom. The reader of the Zohar living in medieval Christian Spain was being firmly admonished to join the battle against those ancient enemies who strengthened the evil forces, wounded or captured the *Shekhinah*, and thus kept the divine light from shining into this world. It does not require a great deal of imagination to understand who these worshipers of darkness must have been, particularly in view of the fact that this was also the era when the Christian image of the Jew as magician and devil-worshiper was first becoming rampant. The Zohar's unstated but clearly present view of

Christianity as sorcery is a mirror reflection of the image of Judaism and Jews that was gaining acceptance throughout the Christian world.

But this is only one side of the picture. As people of deep faith and of great literary and aesthetic sensibility, the Kabbalists could appreciate why Jews were impressed by, and perhaps even attracted to, certain aspects of the Christian story and the religious lives of the large and powerful monastic communities that were so prominent in Christian Spain. The tale of Jesus and his faithful apostles, the passion narrative, and the struggles of the early Church were all powerful and attractive stories. Aspects of Christian theology, including both the complicated oneness of the trinitarian God and the passionate and ever-present devotion to a quasi-divine female figure, made their mark on the kabbalistic imagination. The monastic orders, and especially their commitment to celibacy and poverty, must have been impressive to mystics whose own tradition did not make such demands on them but who shared the medieval otherworldliness that would have highly esteemed such devotion.

The Kabbalists were deeply disconcerted by the power of Christianity to attract Jewish converts, an enterprise that was given high priority particularly by the powerful Dominican order. Much that is found in the Zohar was intended to serve as a counterweight to the potential attractiveness of Christanity to Jews, and perhaps even to the Kabbalists themselves. Of course this should not be seen as an exclusive way of reading the Zohar, a mystical work that was not composed chiefly as a polemical text. Nevertheless, the need to assert Judaism's spirit proudly in the face of triumphalist Christianity stands in the background of the Zohar and should not be ignored as we read it.

The narrative and its setting is the first issue that comes to mind as we examine the Zohar in this light. The tale of a great holy man, Rabbi Shim'on ben Yoḥai, followed by a group of faithful disciples as he wanders about the Holy Land, especially the Galilee, has a familiar ring to it. The Zohar may be seen as proposing the account of this ancient band of Kabbalists as a counter myth to the Gospel tales of Jesus and his apostles. The Zohar's holy men, master and disciples, love one another and shower each other with endless blessings and praises. They also have great supernatural encounters with other holy men, some of them anonymous, who reveal great secrets. The climax of the Zohar narrative, the *Idra Zuta*, is the tale of Rabbi Shim'on's death, preceded by the precisely choreographed assemblage of his faithful disciples. Rabbi Shim'on, like Jesus a figure much associated with the period of Roman persecution of Judaism, dies in ecstasy rather than in martyrdom. But his death casts a dark shadow across the world and his disciples do not know how they will go on without him.

Of course there are differences between the Zohar narrative and that of the Gospels. The influence is subtle and it is impossible to know to what extent it was conscious and to what extent it is simply a carryover of cultural patterns that were so widely accessible (depictions of the Last Supper, for example). Most basically different is the fact that the Zohar's accounts of these wandering holy men always provide the setting for a return to mystical-homiletic interpretations of Scripture. The Zohar narrative in this sense remains addressed to an elite community of Torah scholars. The New Testament apostles were witnesses to miracles; the tales of healing and resurrection in those narratives (themselves modeled on the Elijah-Elisha tales in Hebrew Scripture) had wide appeal and were meant to attract a popular following to the nascent Christian movement. Rabbi Shim'on and his disciples offer surprisingly little by way of such miracles. Their single greatest supernatural act is the disclosure of the secret Torah, a miracle designed to appeal more to the mystical-intellectual elite than to the masses.

The heart of Christian faith lies in the Incarnation, the claim that a specific human being at a particular time in history was in a full sense both God and man, or that God chose to reside wholly in the life, death, and resurrection of this single person. Incarnational faith is seemingly quite far from Judaism, which insists with the psalmist (Ps. 115:16) that "the heavens are the heavens of the Lord; the earth has He given to the children of Adam"; the border between divine and human realms remains quite firmly fixed. In the account of Sinai that stands at the heart of Torah—Judaism's parallel, one might say, to the Incarnation in Christianity—Moses ascends the mountain and returns, still very much man and not God. His shining countenance and the people's inability to look at him give some indication of the Near Eastern tales of apotheosis that lie behind this narrative, but in the Torah the line is not crossed: God is God and man is man. Only in the later midrashic tradition (reflecting on Ps. 90:1, "A Prayer of Moses, the Man of God") are we told, somewhat shockingly to most Jewish ears, that Moses was "half man, half God."[1]

The Zohar remains on the Jewish side of this great theological divide, but comes very close to crossing it. The human *tsaddiq* is an earthly embodiment of the ninth *sefirah* or the *tsaddiq* figure within God. Rabbi Shim'on is the most perfect example of such an earthly *tsaddiq*. He is "the holy lamp," giving light to the Temple above as well as to the earth around him. He embodies both Moses the prophet and Aaron the priest, each of whom may be seen as prefiguring an aspect of his person, the final revealer of those secrets that will allow for the great redemption that is soon to come. Such biblical figures as Moses, Aaron, and King Solomon are regularly depicted in the Zohar as heirophants or mystagogues, priests who perform unfathomable mystery rites that are vital to the world's survival. It is clear that Rabbi Shim'on is the same figure for his own time (and perhaps for all the latter generations) that these men were for theirs. In this way he assumes a role that Rabbi Akiva sometimes plays in rabbinic and *merkavah* sources: that of a latter-day Moses. But both of those figures may be partly shaped as alternatives to the human-divine person of Christianity.

1. Midrash Tehillim, ad loc.

We have referred several times in this essay to the strong erotic element in Kabbalah and especially in the Zohar. The frank and uncensored use of bold sexual language for talking about the inner life of God is a major part of the Zohar's legacy and found throughout the later mystical tradition. Such phrases as "to arouse the feminine waters" or "to serve with a living limb" became so much a part of the conventional language of later Kabbalah that one almost forgets how shocking it is that the divine life is being described in terms of female lubrication or maintaining an erection. How did it happen that such unbridled eroticism was permitted to enter the domain of the sacred? How especially could this have happened in a circle that was at the same time so very cautious and extreme in its views of sexual transgression or temptation?

Use of erotic language to describe the relationship between God and Israel was already well known in biblical times, as witnessed by several of the prophets, especially Hosea. In the rabbinic imagination, the chief vehicle for this all-important metaphor was the Song of Songs, claimed by none other than Rabbi Akiva as the "holy of holies" among the Scriptures.² This assertion assumed an allegorical reading of the Song as describing the love and marriage between God and the community of Israel, an idealized representation of the Jewish people. This collectivist reading of the Canticle dominates throughout the midrashic tradition. Its importance was underscored by the fact that the Christian Church, from the time of Origen, had adopted a parallel interpretation, in which Christ and the *ecclesia* were the lover and beloved of the Song. This Christian allegory was an important vehicle of supersessionist theology; the Church now served as the chosen maiden of divine delight. The Jews, whose rejection by God seemed so obviously confirmed by their historical plight, had a great need to hold fast to the faith that God was their true Lover, the one to whom they cried out even in His seeming absence: "On my bed at night I sought him whom my soul loves"

2. Mishnah Yadayim 3:5.

(Cant. 3:1), knowing in faith that "here he stands behind our wall, peering through the lattice-work, gazing through the windows" (Cant. 2:9).

In the twelfth and thirteenth centuries there was a great shift in the reading of the Song of Songs, from a collectivist to an individualist allegory. The Canticle now came to be seen as a song between God and the soul, a reflection of the new emphasis on individual quest and personal pilgrimage in the religious life of the era. In Christianity this was the development of an old tradition and it especially flourished at the hands of Bernard of Clairvaux and other Cistercians. The Jews were slower to follow this trend, and their few attempts at it were not great successes. The individual Jewish reader (typically a noncelibate male) did not easily see himself as the bride or female beloved of God.

Instead the Jews developed another reading, one that was to reshape Jewish devotional life in a most basic way. If the male Jewish reader could not wax passionate about the erotic relationship between himself and the essentially male figure of God, what was needed was a female presence, inserted between these two males, with whom both could have that passionate relationship. This is exactly what Kabbalah did in placing the female *Shekhinah* at the end of the sefirotic chart or as the gatekeeper between the upper and lower worlds. The inner unity of the Godhead was now seen—especially in Castilian Kabbalah, as we have already noted—primarily in erotic terms. The union of "the blessed Holy One and His *Shekhinah*" became the central focus of all devotional life. But Israel too, as the devoted children, servants, and bridal attendants of the *Shekhinah*, served as "awakeners of her desire to unite with the Holy King." They did this by cultivating their own love for the divine bride in their devoted lives of Torah study and performance of the commandments, including that of holy union with their own wives, an earthly representation of the union above. The presence of this feminine hypostasis opened the gateway to permit the revival of religious passion that so characterizes Kabbalah and especially the community of disciples depicted in the Zohar.

Where did the Jews get this idea of a female intermediary between themselves and God above? It seems quite likely that this is a Jewish adaptation of the cult of the Virgin Mary, very much revived in the Western Church of the twelfth century, especially in France and Spain. Marian piety permeated the culture of Western Europe in this age: the dedication of cathedrals to the Virgin, roadside shrines, passion dramas, music, and art of all forms glorified her role. The Jews surely witnessed this and must have found themselves of two minds about it. On the one hand it would have confirmed their worst impressions of Christianity as pagan, idolatrous, and polytheistic. But there was also something beautiful and tender about the religious life associated with it that could not be ignored. The Jews, whose culture knew no glorification of virginity or celibacy, adapted the notion of a female object of worship to suit their own needs. The notion that there is a divine (or quasi-divine) female presence poised at the entrance to the divine realm, one who loves her children, suffers with them, and accepts their prayers to be brought before the throne of God, is shared by the Marian and kabbalistic traditions. Most likely the latter, which developed in the century following the great Marian revival, is derivative of the former.

Once the female aspect of divinity was in place, without the Christian insistence on virginity, repressed erotic energies could find expression in the spiritual life and strivings of the Kabbalist. In practice, the Zohar's authors indeed represent an especially strict halakhic viewpoint on all sexual matters, one that continued in kabbalistic circles for many centuries. But the gates were thrown wide open to the entrance of rarified and only lightly masked erotic fantasy to fuel the intensity of religious passion. The Kabbalist's self image as *tsaddiq*, the "guardian of the covenant," was, as we have seen, at the same time an image of male potency. His task was to direct the aroused power of his *kavvanah*, or spiritual intention, toward *Shekhinah*, thus stirring the female waters within her so that she aroused, the *tsaddiq* above to unite with her, filling her with the flow of energy from beyond in the form of his male waters, the lights from above as divine semen. As she is filled, the fluid within her overflows to the lower world as well, and the earthly *tsaddiq* receives that blessing. Here the paradigm is of a fully coital expression of sexual union, seemingly closer in some ways to the religion of South India than to the virginal and celibate piety of Christian monks.

But the immediate influence that helped to stir these new energies within Judaism was clearly that of Christianity. If we look again at the kabbalistic chart, especially at the elements highlighted within it by the Castilian Kabbalah, we may see a further parallel to the Christian structures of faith that so characterized this era. *Tif'eret*, or the blessed Holy One, stands at the center; this is the essential figure of the male Deity, the God of the Bible and Jewish tradition. He is flanked on right and left by *Ḥesed* and *Din*, compassion and judgment. This triad of *sefirot* is complemented by *Malkhut* or *Shekhinah* at the lower end of the kabbalistic chart. Together these four *sefirot* constitute a whole, represented by such symbols as the four directions, the four species of Sukkot, the three patriarchs plus King David, and so forth. These are all Jewish symbols of great antiquity. But if we look at this chart *structurally*, we cannot help but notice that it constitutes a trinity, with "God" at the center flanked by two others, with the female "below" them serving as intermediary between heaven and earth, bearer of prayers to God above and birth chamber of divine blessing as it flows into the world. Another kabbalistic configuration imagines *Ḥokhmah* as the Father, *Tif'eret* as the Son, and *Shekhinah* as His bride, to which parallels can also be found in the Christian sources. Because of the second commandment, Jews were held back from any concrete expression of these structures beyond occasional diagrams and charts. But imagine what such kabbalistic images might have looked like in stained glass, for example. There we would have found something indeed very closely parallel to the image-world of medieval Christianity.

It is not at all clear how conscious the Kabbalists themselves were of these patterns of cultural influence. Commonalities of structure that may appear obvious to us from the vantage point of distant centuries may not have been at all clear to those who bore them. Consciously or not, these tremendous importations of spiritual structures were carried out in a subtle and highly creative way, so the connections were far from obvious. Anything less than this would have led to the Kabbalists being labeled heretics and enemies of Judaism, precisely the opposite of their goal, which was to strengthen Judaism in the face of its all-powerful and dangerous rival. It was in part because they were themselves so affected by the attractiveness of Christianity that the authors of the Zohar set out to create a Judaism of renewed mythic power and old-new symbolic forms. Far from being crypto-Christians, they sought to create a more compelling Jewish myth, one that would fortify Jews in resisting Christianity.

An area in which we can clearly see this attempt to put forth a Judaism that stands in direct challenge to Christianity is that of the relationship between marriage and the presence of *Shekhinah* or the Holy Spirit. The culture of Christian Spain in the thirteenth century was highly monastic. The time of the Zohar was the great heyday of both Dominican and Franciscan spirituality, and these and other orders played a great role in the socioeconomic as well as the religious life of the surrounding culture. While Judaism contained neither a tradition of monasticism nor a glorification of celibacy, the great monastic establishments must have been impressive to Jewish pietists, who did share in some of the values represented by the monkish life. Scholars have long noted the influence of Christian monasticism (especially its glorification of poverty) on circles close to the Zohar. In sharp contrast to the Christian glorification of celibacy, the Zohar insists (with relatively meager support in earlier Jewish sources) that an unmarried man is merely half a person and that the *Shekhinah* does not dwell where the wholeness of male-female union is lacking. When a man is away from his wife, the Zohar tells us—whether he is traveling, busy studying Torah with his companions, or prevented from union with her because of her menstrual impurity—the *Shekhinah* joins to him, becoming his female spiritual companion. But she does so only by merit of the fact that he has an earthly female partner to whom he will return in holy union. Anyone who has no wife cannot expect that the presence of God will be joined to him. Moses is the sole exception to this rule. The Zohar's insistence on the spiritual necessity of marriage can best be understood, relative to Castile of the thirteenth century, as a frontal attack on Christian monasticism, focusing its claim precisely where it would hurt most. Abstinence from marriage, claims the Zohar, does not free one for marriage to God, as the monks would have it; rather, celibacy makes it impossible for one to contain the presence of the Holy Spirit.

The relationship of the Kabbalah and the Zohar to the surrounding Christian culture was thus highly ambivalent and complex. The resentment that the Jews naturally bore as an oppressed and taunted minority is very much present in the outcries of the Zohar's speakers against the wicked nations. From a formal theological and halakhic point of view, the Zohar offers not the slightest leniency in its attitude toward Christianity or any other non-Jewish religion. But operating as it did on the plane of myth and imagination, the Zohar absorbed subtle cultural influences and structures of thought that were current in the surrounding culture. The Zohar is very much a reflection of Judaism in the setting of the medieval Christian West, shaped by a unique interweaving of resentment, attraction, and creative adaptation.

Part III

SELECTED THEMES

WITHIN THE ZOHAR

The purpose of the following brief sections is not to offer a complete outline of the Zohar's views on these key theological topics. The Zohar is a vast and nonsystematic work, and a wide range of opinions is presented within it, especially when various subsections of the Zohar are considered. The remarks in the following chapters are meant rather to help prepare the reader who will encounter these points within the Zohar text and would like a brief reference to them.

8

Creation and Origins

The Zohar devotes a great deal of attention to Creation and the origins of existence. In this the Zohar shows itself to be very much connected to the world of medieval Jewish philosophy, in which Creation was seen to be a central theological issue. Unlike the early rabbis, whose primary theological focus had been on revelation and the chain of authority, the medievals viewed religion through the lens of the Middle Ages' "cosmic spirituality." This was an orientation that saw philosophical, scientific, and religious knowledge as belonging to a single whole. A growing scientific awareness of the vastness of the universe combined with Aristotelian and Neoplatonic metaphysics to depict a wondrous multitiered cosmos radiating out from a divine center. The material world was the lowest rung of that hierarchy of being and only the palest reflection of the single source that animated all of existence. Knowledge of God was better obtained by an understanding of the universe as a whole, with concentration on the upper, immaterial spheres. God was glorified by the grandeur of that entire universe and by the beauty and wisdom of the natural law that governed it. Speculation on the origin and nature of that cosmos was seen by the medievals as essential to the quest for wisdom or truth. This characteristic of medieval thought transcends the lines between religious traditions as well as any distinction one can make between "philosophers" and "mystics."

While this shift in emphasis from the rabbinic to the kabbalistic imagination took place under the aegis of medieval philosophical speculation, the Zohar typically seeks to ground its views in a biblical rather than a contemporary context. For this it turns to the legacy of the prophets and psalmists, who were so often enthralled with the wonders of Creation, depicting them as witnesses to the Creator's wondrous power. Verses from Isaiah, the Psalms, and Job are widely quoted in the Zohar, whose authors' thorough familiarity with even the most obscure parts of Scripture indeed rivaled that of the ancient midrashic masters. These verses bring to the Zohar a powerful evocative *poesis*, rooted in their original meaning, while dissecting and reweaving them to hint at the *upper* Creation, the realm of kabbalistic mystery.

In the context of medieval philosophy, it is not surprising that the Zohar deals with cosmic origins primarily on the inner divine level. It is the emergence of the *sefirot* from *Ein Sof* and the resulting constitution of the divine *persona* that captures most of the Zohar's attention. The lower Creation, that of actual corporeal existence, seems almost unworthy of discussion, and indeed is treated only somewhat cursorily by the Zohar. But there are some important theological reasons for this choice and omission. These require further discussion here.

The questions of God (proofs of God's existence, the nature of God and divine "attributes") and Creation were deeply intertwined in the medieval theological mind. Creation was used by Maimonides and others as a basis for belief in God, the Unmoved Mover or the primary force that lies behind all chains of cause and effect. This God, however, is an abstraction or a logical principle, whether derived through Aristotelian arguments of cause and effect or through Neoplatonic reflections on the prime source of spiritual energy or "light" and the successively dimmer reflections of it through the universe. Philosophers in both schools struggled mightily with the question of *willful* Creation. Does existence flow naturally out the cosmic Source into all of being? Did God choose to create the world, or does it simply exist by dint of God's own nature? There is a great and unresolved distance between these Hellenically rooted philosophical speculations and the God of Israel, the supreme Person of the biblical-rabbinic tradition, Who creates by an act of supreme and absolute will, for the sake of Israel, Torah, or the righteous who are to inhabit His earth and bring Him pleasure.

The philosophers, especially Maimonides, had found ways to dismiss this earlier and more personified view of God, seeing it (since they continued to view Torah as divine revelation and thus had to account for the Torah's depiction of God) as some combination of a concession to the primitive thinking of the ancients and a divinely given educational tool to effect moral behavior among the masses. Much of the first section of the *Guide for the Perplexed* is devoted to a treatment of biblical language that serves to undermine the naive theology of biblical literalism. The God of philosophy was indeed the Source of Sources or the Unmoved Mover, but endowed with just enough of will and consciousness to meet the needs of Judaism as recast in the philosophical mode. The fact that there might exist within this framework, as there surely did for Maimonides, a highly refined form of religious passion and devotion to God's service, was lost on all but the most careful of readers.

The Kabbalists were utterly opposed to this theological stance. For them, the God of the rabbinic tradition was very much alive. They affirmed not only willful Creation, but Creation for the sake of Israel and the souls of the righteous. They turned back to the fragmentary cosmogenic myths found in ancient sources, both in classical Midrash and in some aggadic works bordering on the *merkavah* tradition, and wove them into their own system of kabbalistic speculation. In fact, a large part of their inspiration came from the seemingly most bizarre corners of the earlier Jewish theological imagination. They were unwilling to join with the philosophers in dismissing the mythical and folk elements of Jewish piety that had such a strong hold on the popular religious mind. At the same time, their own mystical speculations had led them down the path of abstraction. The Kabbalists' *Ein Sof*, the endless and undefined source of existence, was very like the object of the philosophers' pure contemplation. The tension between the abstract One of Ones that underlies both philosophy and mysticism and the personified God of Jewish myth and imagination remained unresolved for the philosophers. For the Kabbalists, it stood as a great challenge.

It is in part for this reason that the Zohar's treatment of Creation concentrates mostly on the inner divine process. Much of the Zohar may be seen as an attempt to discover how the personal and anthropomorphic God came forth out of the recesses of mysterious oneness. Described in some of the Zohar's most poetic and imaginative passages as theogonic process, the emergence of "God" from the hidden Godhead, this treatment may also be viewed as the Kabbalists' way of resolving the tension between their own mysticism and their deep commitment to the personalist and mythical elements of the ancient Jewish legacy. The real story of Creation therefore has to be that of the "birth" of God, the personified Father (and Mother, in this case) of the universe. How that God then brought forth the lower, material word is only of secondary interest. In good Neoplatonic fashion, the lower universe is depicted as structurally parallel to, yet a pale imitation of, the upper one. The relationship between these "upper" and "lower" stages of Creation is described by Gershom Scholem:

> Theogony and cosmogony represent not two different acts of creation, but two aspects of the same. On every plane—in the world of the Merkabah and the angels, which is below the Sefiroth, in the various heavens, and in the world of the four elements—creation mirrors the inner movement of the divine life. The "vestiges" of the innermost re-

ality are present even in the most external of things. Everywhere there is the same rhythm, the same motion of the waves. The act which results beyond and above time in the transformation of the hidden into the manifest God is paralleled in the time-bound reality of every other world. Creation is nothing but an external development of these forces which are active and alive in God Himself. Nowhere is there a break, a discontinuity. . . . The most frequent illustration of this doctrine . . . is that of the chain and the links of which it consists. There are in this chain, the links of which are represented by the totality of the different worlds, different grades of links, some deeply hidden and some visible from outside, but there is no such thing as isolated existence.[1]

Here we may see another reason that the Zohar says little about the emergence of the lower world. The kabbalistic system, by its very nature, is one of emanation, of existence flowing forth from a source, both in its origins and in its daily renewal. For the lower world that source is *Malkhut,* or the union of the *sefirot* culminating in *Malkhut,* that allows for the "birth" of souls and the overflow of bounty that sustains existence. Life is the result of this outpouring of energy from *Malkhut,* very much affected, as we shall see later, by the course of human actions. The relationship between God and world in this sort of faith is essentially not that of Creator and Creation, indicating a true separation between God and the universe, but rather one of inner core and outward manifestations. The "lower" world is in fact a "vessel" or a "garment" to contain that radiating energy. The divine Self emanates through the universe and is revealed, paradoxically, as it is "garbed" in each of the many creatures that inhabit it.

This theology of emanation implies a degree of pantheism. The language of the Zohar, to be sure, is that of Creation, even the morally determined and willful Creation of rabbinic tradition. Behind this terminology of Creation, however, stands a dynamic indwelling God whose presence pulsates through the entire cosmos. But pantheism has impor-

1. Scholem, *Major Trends in Jewish Mysticism* (New York: Schocken Books, 1941), p. 223.

tant and potentially problematic theological ramifications. The "otherness" of God is called into question if God underlies and animates all that is. Such issues as moral responsibility and divine punishment might require reexamination in the context of an emanation-centered theology. The Kabbalists, a morally conservative group within the Jewish community, sought to keep these questions under wraps. Opposing philosophy as champions of traditional faith, the role in which they had cast themselves, they surely did not want the dangers of their own theological position to make them the object of new controversy. For this reason too they kept their discussions about the emergence of the lower worlds quite vague, avoiding any specific treatment of the sublunar creatures' relationship to the sefirotic universe out of which they came and in whose image they were formed.

In fact, the Zohar reflects a form of Kabbalah that throroughly if inconsistently combines emanationist and personalist views of the relationship between God, world, and humanity. It is from the overflow of grace, the bounteous *shefa* pouring forth in moments of divine union, that souls are born and that the world is sustained. But this bounty derives from the coupling of the male and female *sefirot*, essentially the sacred marriage of *Tif'eret* and *Malkhut*, which can take place only through the stirring aroused by Israel. It is their good deeds and longings for God, as we shall see later in our discussion of the commandments, that arouse the "feminine waters" within *Malkhut* to call forth and awaken the love of her (and Israel's) divine Partner. The emanational flow is thus made dependent upon an act of divine will, depicted in the form of eros, a personalist passion that is as much inner drive as it is response to specific human actions.

The Zohar's focus on the inner divine aspects of Creation allows it to shift the meaning of certain key terms and symbols. The philosophers' insistence on *creatio ex nihilio, yesh me-ayin* in Hebrew, was completely reinterpreted in sefirotic terms. *Keter*, also called *ayin* or divine

"Nothingness," is now the "nothing" out of which Creation comes. The Kabbalists tirelessly quote Job 28:1 in this context: *ve-ha-hokhmah me-ayin timmatse*. Rather than reading it interrogatively as "Whence does wisdom come?" they interpret it as a statement: "Wisdom (*Hokhmah*) comes from Nothing (*ayin*)." The six days of Creation, the framework of the opening chapter of Genesis, are also transferred to the sefirotic realm, representing the six *sefirot* from *Hesed* to *Yesod*, culminating in *Malkhut*, the bride who is their Sabbath. Even such terms as "upper world" and "lower world" are used internally in the sefirotic descriptions, referring to *Binah* and *Malkhut*. Often it is not clear when this is the case and when the Zohar is actually referring to the *lower* world of material existence. "Earth" (*adamah*) and "land" (*erets*) are also symbol-terms for the *Shekhinah*, again complicating the discussion.

When the Zohar does refer to the creation of this world, it does so by combining three networks of mythical symbolism. One is the language of birth, to which we have already referred. *Shekhinah* giving birth to the lower worlds may be the "lower mother" or the "hind of dawn." In some passages, Her painful birthing may involve some compromise with the forces of darkness, thus giving them a degree of power over the emergent lower realms of being. Human souls in particular are spoken of as being "born" of *Shekhinah*, bearing within themselves the stamp of the sefirotic world that is the Zohar's understanding of Creation "in God's image."

Another set of symbols goes back to Genesis' image of Creation through the power of divine speech ("God said, 'Let there be . . .' and there was . . ."). The Kabbalist exults in the notion that God creates the world through some supernal and mysterious manifestation of language. This may take the form of permutation of letters, in the tradition of *Sefer Yetsirah*, the uttering of mysterious divine names, or some other aspect of verbal self-revelation. A key symbol for the emergence of the *sefirot* is the movement within God from thought (*Hokhmah* and

Binah) to voice (*Tif'eret*) to speech (*Malkhut*). This to say that Creation is a form of divine self-articulation. The revelation of the Torah, as we shall see, is a repetition or an externalization of this inner divine process.

A third mythical element has to do with the ancient legacy of pictorial depictions of Creation. These *aggadot*, preserved most vividly in the opening chapters of the eighth-century Midrash *Pirkei de-Rabbi Eliezer*, were well known to the Zohar's authors and they used them in an expansive and creative way. Some *aggadot* tell of elements that preexisted Creation, while others, preserving fragments of pre-Israelite mythology, tell of forces opposed to Creation that had to be slain or defeated so that Creation might come forth. These become constituent elements of the Zohar's demonic universe, playing a significant role in the Zohar's repeated and highly colorful descriptions of Creation.

9

Between Worlds

The Kabbalist inhabits a cosmos of interlocking and interpenetrating realms. The physical structures of the "lower world" reflect the dynamics of "higher" spiritual worlds and embody their energies. "Above" and "below" exist in an analogical relationship to each other. The lower world is sustained by the emanatory flow from the upper world, one that is increased or lessened in response to human actions. But the lower world is also a reflection of the world above or behind it. Just as the *sefirot* both hide and reveal the light that flows into them (one that could not come to be known except through them), so too does the lower world both hide and disclose the power and the structure of the *sefirot* that underlie it.

The vertical and hierarchical model on which the medieval universe is structured underlies the entire Zohar. *Upper world* and *lower world*, terms used with great frequency throughout the work, are both parallel and interdependent. At times the phrase "upper world" refers to the sefirotic realm as a whole, as parallel to the "lower world" that is the concrete universe of human action. But elsewhere the upper and lower worlds may reflect an intradivine distinction. Most commonly these are

Binah and *Malkhut*, the two "female" realms into which a divine force enters. But the terms *upper* and *lower* may also refer to any number of other distinctions, including those between *Shekhinah* and Her heavenly hosts, between *Tif'eret* and *Malkhut*, between the three highest *sefirot* and the seven others, and so forth. In fact, it is often both impossible and unnecessary to know just which "address" is intended, since the claim applies to all the upper and lower realms at once. Such is the way of the Zohar's worldview that it sees each realm as part of the great hierarchical system, fully linked to all those above and below it.

This way of seeing the world *be-aspeklaria shel ma'alah*, or from an upper-world perspective, is held to be true regarding both of the primary dimensions by which the lower world is measured: time and space. The passage of time—days, years, eons—points beyond time itself to the world of the *sefirot*. The days of the week are the seven lower *sefirot* in earthly incarnation. This perception is cultivated particularly in the extensive reflections on the Sabbath found throughout the Zohar. Celebrating or "entering into" the Sabbath is in effect partaking of *Shekhinah*, entering into that cosmic and transtemporal realm that is replete with God's presence. With regard to space, the six *sefirot* above *Shekhinah* are regularly referred to as the "six extensions," encompassing within them all of primal "space." Sometimes the four key *sefirot*, *Ḥesed-Gevurah-Tif'eret-Malkhut*, are symbolically represented by the four directions, again giving the sense that all of primal space is included within them. The influence of the *Sefer Yetsirah* tradition is particularly to be felt here, as the *sefirot* are referred to as "the deep structure" of all reality.

Hierarchically "below" the ten *sefirot* in the Zohar's cosmology is a series of *heikhalot*, or "palaces." These are intermediary chambers of divine radiance, arranged in the pattern (mostly) of the seven lower *sefirot*. The *heikhalot* are described in several sections of the Zohar in highly experiential and ecstatic terms. While these *heikhalot* are set forth with great pomp and enthusiasm, the journey through them is given a role subordinate to contemplation of the *sefirot*, on which the Zohar's main energies are focused. The *heikhalot* are in fact used in part to show how the sefirotic structure extends beyond the Godhead and is repeated throughout the lower forms of existence.

Kabbalists more or less contemporaneous with the authors of the Zohar had begun to describe a four-tiered universe, with the successive "worlds" denoted by the terms *atsilut* ("emanation"), *beri'ah* ("creation"), *yetsirah* ("formation"), and *asiyyah* ("fashioning"). These terms respectively referred to the inner divine realm; the world of visionary experience, including the divine throne and the *heikhalot*; the realm of the angels; and the world of souls. The material world was taken to be lower than *assiyah* but dominated by its spirit. Each of the four worlds was structured in the same tenfold pattern of the *sefirot*. For reasons unknown to us, the Zohar refrains from using this system, leaving the intermediary and angelic universes with no clear pattern of organization beyond that of the *heikhalot* themselves. The poetic spirit in which the Zohar is written seems better fulfilled by vast hosts of angels rushing about the universe, often counted in fantastic and seemingly arbitrary numbers, than by the more "systematic" angelologies and structured cosmologies described by others.

Also absent from the Zohar is speculation on the cosmic jubilee and the return of all being to its origins in *Binah* at the culmination of a great 49,000 year cycle. Kabbalists before the Zohar, including Naḥmanides, referred to this matter as one of special secrecy, to be taught only in the most esoteric of mystical circles. On the basis of a Talmudic *aggadah* that said, "The world exists for six thousand years: two thousand chaos, two thousand Torah, and two thousand messianic times,"[1] the mystics imagined a seventh millennium in which earthly existence would cease, a spiritualized "world that is wholly Sabbath."

1. Sanhedrin 97a.

They then counted seven such sabbatical aeons, each under the aegis of a particular *sefirah*. These were to culminate in a cosmic jubilee, in which all being was to return to its source in the womb of *Binah*, thence presumably to be born again into another series of sabbaths. It is unknown to us why the Zohar's authors chose to ignore (aside from occasional possible hints) both of these key tools of kabbalistic cosmological speculation. Further investigation of this matter may prove fruitful in characterizing the particular mystical circle out of which these writings emerged.

The natural world is seen by the Zohar to contain a great many phenomena that point to the supernal structure. The relationship of heaven and earth, and of sun and moon, the way rivers flow into the sea, the growth of trees due to sunlight and water—all of these are seen as earthly replications of the sefirotic pattern. There is an embrace of nature in the Zohar that sees it as a manifestation of divine reality. Some of this is presented as an enthusiastic renewal of the psalmist's exultation in the wonders of God's creation. But as the Zohar unravels its exegetical interest in the biblical descriptions of Creation, it is often these structural parallels between upper and lower worlds that it seeks to uncover.

The most important earthly representations of the cosmic structure in the Zohar are to be found in the Tabernacle-Temple and the human being, particularly the soul. In both of these cases, the Zohar builds on older midrashic traditions that saw soul or Temple as microcosm or earthly reflection of the divine reality. The Zohar adapts these typologies to its own symbolic structure, one based on, but going far beyond, that which is found in the rabbinic tradition.

The origins of the Zohar's hierarchical worldview reach back into the depths of Israel's mythical imagination, and perhaps even into ancient pre-Israelite structures of thought. The notion that the earthly Temple stands parallel to the heavenly Temple that is God's true dwelling is well attested by both biblical and midrashic texts. Even a triple-tiered universe, with the Temple standing over the opening to the nether-world as well as at the gateway to the heavens, is documented in early sources. The extended wings of the two cherubim over the ark in Moses' Tabernacle seem to form a "seat" for the divine Glory (*kavod* in the Bible, *shekhinah* in the rabbinic sources), a presence that extends downward from its home above. Human actions, according to well-known Midrashim, cause that presence either to be present in this world or to retreat up its own inner ladder to the seventh heaven, far from the sullied realms below. All of this stands in the background of the Zohar's own more elaborately constructed cosmological vision.

The human being as an earthly embodiment of the divine structure also plays a major role in the Zohar's religious worldview. Kabbalah represents a highly anthropocentric version of Judaism, especially in contrast to the more theocentric views of the medieval Jewish philosophers. It sees the world as having been created for the sake of humanity, and the person as a locus of divine energy, playing a vital role in the maintenance of the entire cosmos. Humans were created in the divine image in order to fulfill this purpose. This view of humanity is manifest in the Zohar's perspectives on both soul and body.

The Zohar speaks frequently of three parts of the soul, designated by the terms *nefesh*, *ruah*, and *neshamah* (literally but inadequately rendered as "self," "spirit," and "breath"). The tripartite division of the human soul was widespread in medieval intellectual circles, based on notions first developed by Plato and Aristotle. Discussion of various aspects of the human soul, or even multiple souls within the person, is found in earlier Jewish philosophical and mystical writings. But the linkage made in the Zohar between these three terms and specific (if sometimes variable) loci within the sefirotic world seems to be original. Most Zohar discussions link *nefesh*, the lowest and most universally shared rung of soul, to *Malkhut*, the *sefirah* from which souls are born.

Ruah is parallel to *Tif'eret*, the divine male principle whose union with *Malkhut* brings about that birth. *Neshamah*, sometimes said to belong only to the righteous, represents the mysterious rung of *Binah*, pointing to the unknowable realms beyond.[2] Some passages also refer to two higher aspects of soul, *hayyah* and *yehidah*, a theme taken up by later Kabbalists influenced by the Zohar.

The analogy between the soul and the sefirotic universe bears with it implications that lead in two directions. One is the sense that true self-knowledge leads to the knowledge of God, also a widespread belief in the medieval world. Turning inward to contemplate the self and its origins was an important part of kabbalistic knowledge. The other implication is more in the direction of theurgy, or the potential effect of human actions on the divine world. The soul *partakes* of the divine structure in a real way. It is not just a copy of the *sefirot*, but actually represents their presence within the self. Because of this, the actions of the person, including both the sanctification and the defilement of the soul, make their mark above. The interrelationship between God and person is quite mutual; the parts of the soul both show their divine origins and allow for the possibility of human action on the cosmic plane.

The human body as well as the soul reflects the divine image. This is a unique view of the Kabbalists in the medieval Jewish context, one that generally shared in the Platonically inspired denigration of "coarse matter," and with it all things physical. The fact that the *sefirot* are usually depicted in a chart that corresponds to the human body lends the latter a symbolic dignity that is quite striking. It is because of this likeness to the supernal realm that the body can serve as a vehicle for the uplifting of sacred energies and the restoration of the divine cosmos. The Zohar is fascinated by the possibility of using parts of the body for

2. The Zoharic discussion of the soul, its parts, and its origin is particularly complex. Here the treatment by Tishby, *Wisdom of the Zohar*, pp. 677–722, is especially recommended.

sacred purposes. Such acts as raising one's hands in blessing or opening the mouth in prayer are subjects for deep reflection and discourse among the companions. Such bodily phenomena as the coursing of blood through the veins or (according to Galenic medicine) the flow of semen from the brain, through the spine, and into the phallus, are depicted as earthly analogies to mysterious divine processes. Of course it is also possible to read the analogy in the reverse, suggesting that these biological phenomena lent to the Kabbalists a certain view of processes in the upper world. All of this is part of the union of sciences (in the broadest sense, culminating in religion) widely accepted in the Middle Ages.

Alongside these passages that glorify the body by analogy to the divine, the Zohar also contains vivid descriptions of the dangers of bodily temptations and hints that demonic elements may have had a hand in the formation of the physical body itself. This conflict of views shows the deep ambivalence with which bodily matters were seen by the Kabbalists of the thirteenth century. This is especially true with regard to sexuality. The Zohar contains glorious descriptions of the correspondence between the upper union and the lower union, assuring the reader than his coupling with his wife, carried out within the proper halakhic rules and bounded as well by mystical intention, is potentially a holy and cosmos-redeeming act, one that unites the *sefirot* and draws a holy soul to come into this world. But that same deed, or even the temptation to think of it, outside those bounds of propriety, is condemned in the fiercest terms imaginable. This terror of sexual sin and the damage it can do to the cosmic structure was an important part of the Zohar's legacy to later forms of kabbalistic praxis.

IO

Evil and the Demonic

We have seen that the Zohar's theology is an attempt to tame and reconcile several competing and even contradictory insights and experiences. The Kabbalists were true mystics, aware of the oneness underlying and uniting all discrete phenomena. They were influenced profoundly by their own inner pneumatic experiences and by the metaphysics bequeathed to them by their Neoplatonic predecessors. But as medieval Jews, they were also members of an exiled and oppressed community. They were thus uniquely sensitive to the undeniable reality of evil in the world and the horrors of history. These too needed to find an outlet in their very personally expressive writings, despite their seeming threat to the harmonic unity of being. The tension between the sublime vision of sefirotic unity, resulting in light and bliss throughout the worlds, and the reality of darkness and oppression colors almost every page of the Zohar. As noted earlier, the work is distinguished as well by a second tension, deriving from an attraction to an abstract contemplative mysticism combined with a powerful mythical imagination. The latter expressed itself in a set of potent and sometimes frightening symbols. Much of the kabbalistic *ouevre* can be interpreted as the product of an inner dialectic around these two tensions. Nowhere is this more clearly felt than in the Zohar's treatment of evil and the demonic realm.

By its very nature, mysticism bears within it a monist strain in theology. The mystic seeks to uncover the ultimate oneness of all being and to experience some taste of that primal truth. The theology that accompanies this attempt is hard-pressed to deal with the reality of evil. If all existence is a reflection of divinity, what is evil's place? Generally there have been two tendencies in dealing with this problem, as is true within Western theology more generally. One approach, often associated with Neoplatonism, is the denial of evil as real. What seems to be evil is in fact illusion, ignorance, or distance from the ever-shining divine light. When we become enlightened, closer to God, evil will disappear from before us. The other approach is the path of Gnosticism, differing sharply from Neoplatonism in this area. Evil is here depicted as real and frightening. Some compromise with dualism is needed to explain its origin and continued existence. Yes, God is the one source of all that is. But somehow in the transmission of that divine presence into its this-worldly garb there has been a tragic fault or flaw, a rebellion within the lesser cosmic forces, or perhaps an unwillingness of the lower worlds to receive God's light, allowing the forces of evil to exist, and even to achieve awesome power.

Both of these approaches are to be found in the Zohar. The former view, largely that of the earlier Gerona Kabbalists, is manifest in depictions of evil as a pale imitation of the sefirotic realm. Indeed, it bears the same tenfold structure as the world of divinity, but it is a mere shadow, a mocking imitation of the divine realm. This illusory world has power only over those foolish enough to take it for true. The latter view, certainly dominant within the Zohar, links that work to the circle of "Gnostic" Kabbalists active in Castile in the mid-thirteenth century, especially to the writings of Isaac of Soria and Moses of Burgos.

Out of Isaac of Soria's teaching, the Zohar developed a vision of the
"*Sitra Aḥara*"—"the Other Side"—which plays a significant role in the
Zoharic mythos. In one of its most powerful set of images, the Zohar
describes the *Sitra Aḥara* as a series of *qelippot*, four interlocking "shells"
surrounding the realm of divinity and constituting a "side" of impurity.
The image of the shell, surrounding and protecting the inner content
of a particular divine constellation, was part of the older kabbalistic
legacy. But in the Zohar these shells take on the frightening countenance of actively demonic forces. The names of these *qelippot*—"stormy
wind," "huge cloud," "flashing fire," and "radiance"—were derived from
the blustery conflagration envisioned by Ezekiel as surrounding the Divine Chariot. "I looked, and lo, a stormy wind came sweeping out of
the north—a huge cloud and flashing fire, surrounded by a radiance"
(Ez. 1:4). "Radiance" (*Nogah*), the shell closest to the worlds of divinity,
is viewed as a mixture of good and evil, capable of interaction with Divinity. The innermost core of the *Sitra Aḥara*, "Stormy Wind" (*Ruaḥ
Se'arah*) is a domain of unalloyed defilement.

Constrained to account for the way this highly pictorialized demonic realm exists in a universe where all comes forth from *Ein Sof*,
the Zohar presents two distinct pictures of the *Sitra Aḥara*'s origins.
Most prevelant is the image of the Other Side as the fiery dross emit-
ted by *Gevurah* at the moment of its emanation. Some passages describe this in terms of the tension between *Ḥesed* and *Gevurah* discussed earlier. Other texts see it as an act of purgation, as God casting
the roots of anger and harshness out of the emergent divine Self. Having been forcibly, even violently, removed from the realm of divinity,
this dross reconstitutes itself as the forces of the demonic Other. This
vision was derived from the teachings of Rabbi Moses of Burgos. A
second vision, enunciated in hints and veiled allusions, goes beyond
even the teachings of Rabbi Isaac in its radicality. It uses the Torah's
account of the genealogy of the Edomite kings (Gen. 36:31 ff.), who

"reigned and died before there was a king in Israel." These "kings that died" are taken by the Zohar to allude to a set of primordial, purgative expulsions of negative energy from the depths of *Keter*, preceding even the very beginning of the ordered sefirotic emanation. Only this removal of the dross at the highest level cleared the way for the proper revelation of the sefirotic potencies. Its origin in this highest and most recondite divine realm accounts for the great and mysterious power the Zohar attributes to the demonic.

These explanations of evil's origins within the divine world in part serve the role of apologetics, assuring the concerned reader that belief in the Other Side is not as profoundly dualistic as it might first appear. But this is not the primary way they should be read. Out of the works of the "Gnostic" Kabbalists the Zohar's authors have constructed a vivid mythology of evil, one in which they and their original intended readers thoroughly believed. They saw both cosmos and soul as the battleground in an eternal struggle between two contending cosmic forces, one that will not be finally resolved until the end of time. There are passages in the Zohar that recall the tone, and even some of the specific imagery, of the Jewish apocalypses of the first and second centuries. Yet like all other aspects of reality, the Other Side originates within divinity, is animated by a divine spark, and yearns to ascend back to its source. When all worlds, above and below, exist in a state of perfect balance and harmony, the Other Side is under the firm control of the *sefirot* and plays a positive role in the management of the world, functioning as an obedient punishing rod of divine justice. However, when the worlds are askew and imbalanced, *Sitra Aḥara* develops an independent will. In its quest for an autonomous life fueled by divine light and energy, it oversteps its bounds and strives to usurp the place of *Tif'eret* or *Yesod* in the holy union, snatching the *Shekhinah* and the world from His embrace in an act described quite vividly as abduction or even rape. The great moments of redemption enumerated in the biblical history of salvation belong as much to the *Shekhinah* as to Israel, with redemption occurring both above and below. Israel's human enemies and oppressors, such as Esau, Pharoah, and Amalek, are but the phenomenal agents of a far greater and more dangerous cosmic foe.

In describing this ongoing battle against evil, the mythical, mystical, and moralistic elements of the Zohar all work in tandem and indeed are inseparable from one another. The often personified embodiments of wickedness—Samael, chief of the demons; his consort Lilit, or Na'amah; and all their hosts—are depicted with great color in many places within the Zohar. Images abound of the primordial serpent and the great sea monster floating through ten rivers of defilement. These all set about the task of leading humans into sin. Indeed this mission is vital to them, for it is only through the energy released to them in acts of human transgression that they receive the life-energy they need to sustain themselves. Cut off from adequate sustenance by their divine source, the forces of evil are powerless unless given energy from "below."

The only bulwark that stands against these antidivine forces and their utter dominance of the world is that of Israel, and especially of the righteous among them. Every good deed they do, every commandment they fulfill or prayer they offer with the proper mystical intent, serves to awaken the *Shekhinah*. She unites with her spouse, is energized by Him, and they together become mighty warriors in the battle against evil. They are more powerful than their wicked counterparts and ultimate victory will surely belong to them. But they will be able to claim that victory only when the merit of human goodness clearly outweighs the burden of human evil, a condition against which all the forces of evil and temptation are arrayed.

Sometimes it is clear that the battle cannot be won, that evil is stronger than goodness in the present world. Then it is possible, through certain prescriptions of the Torah, to either "bribe" or fool evil (Samael is sometimes described as "an old and foolish king") to keep it from destroying those vital points of goodness that do exist. Such sacrifices as the Yom Kippur scapegoat or the monthly sin offering exist for that purpose. The chief of the demons here becomes something of a desert scavenger, so busy devouring the meager meal he has been given that he fails to notice the righteous, who are meanwhile uplifting whole universes of goodness and saving them from his grasp.

I I

Torah and Revelation

As faithful Jews, the Kabbalists were firm believers in the revelation of the Torah. The day of the event at Sinai was taken, alongside those of the erection of the Tabernacle and the Temple, as the apex of human history. The rich legacy of rabbinic legends and *theologoumena* set out to glorify Torah and its revelation were fully embraced by the Kabbalists. They enthusiastically affirmed that every letter, vowel point, and musical notation in the Torah was of divine origin. The Torah given to Moses at Sinai was an embodiment of the primordial Torah, which existed with God before Creation and which He consulted in making the world. This view stood in great contrast to the reservations placed by the Jewish rationalists of the Middle Ages on certain aspects of Torah, including both its seemingly naive view of prophecy, its many accounts of miracles, and its anthropomorphic views of God. While they too formally accepted the literal belief in Sinaitic revelation as dogma, their efforts at reinterpreting or even "purifying" concepts expressed in the Torah text led away from literalism and toward what has been characterized as a protocritical approach to reading the scriptural text. Here as in other areas the Kabbalists donned the mantle of theological orthodoxy, depicting themselves as great defenders of ancient tradition, reaching all the way back to Sinai itself.

Despite their protestations at the reinterpretations of others, however, the Kabbalists were far from literalists. While they did defend the literal truth claims of the biblical and rabbinic sources, they, like the philosophers, were interested primarily in a deeper reading of the text, one often thought of as "esoteric" in both intellectual camps. The Kabbalists developed this way of reading much more thoroughly, however, and were able to find secret meanings even in the seemingly most obscure or insignificant portions of the Torah. The very fact that many of the important works of Kabbalah, including the Zohar, took the form of commentaries on the Torah (unlike the major writings of the philosophers, which were chiefly independent treatises) opened the way toward a deeper integration of kabbalistic thinking and the interpretive project. The nature of the secret truth that this deeper exegesis was to find also distinguished Kabbalah from philosophy. The latter sought to learn scientific and metaphysical truth, often in the Aristotelian mode, from the study of Scripture. This was at best a difficult, even somewhat tortured, enterprise. The Kabbalist sought allusions everywhere to the secret inner life of God. But the language of those allusions, thanks both to the flexibility and to the deep Jewishness of sefirotic language, indeed often made one feel that they sprang directly from the Torah text. In this way Kabbalah succeeded in capturing the imagination of Jewry, while philosophy retained the air of a burden forced upon it from without.

The Zohar is interested in three levels of Torah, associated with three rungs of the sefirotic mysteries. The primordial Torah corresponds to *Ḥokhmah*, the written Torah to *Tif'eret*, and the oral Torah or the interpretive tradition to *Malkhut*. Many passages treat these three aspects of Torah as parallel but distinct entities. The correspondences between them reflect the parallels the Zohar frequently finds between "upper worlds" and "lower worlds," or various levels of the sefirotic structure.

But there is also a view expressed in some places that understands the three as stages in a single process of divine self-disclosure. Here the primordial Torah is depicted as *mahashavah*, the innermost "thought" or mind of God. This Torah is the original plan or inner map of the universe within the divine mind. The flow from *Hokhmah* to *Tif'eret*, or the revelation of the primordial Torah as that of Sinai, happens at the level of *qol*, where "voice" is joined to God's thought, allowing for articulation. But this act of divine speech is not yet complete, for it is hardly accessible to the human ear. (Indeed the word *qol* in the account of revelation in Exodus 19–20 may be rendered "thunderclap" more readily than "voice" in the human sense.) Only at the level of *Malkhut*, or when the interpretive tradition is linked to the written Torah, does the voice of God truly emerge in *dibbur* or "speech." This corresponds to the classic rabbinic (and in the medieval context, anti-Karaitic) view that the written Torah can be understood and followed *only* through the authoritative chain of interpretation.

Creation and Revelation are thus seen by the Zohar as twin processes of divine self-disclosure, the emergence of God from hiddenness. Just as the divine presence, in the form of sefirotic structure, is "garbed" in all of Creation, so too is it found in the written and oral Torah. Like Creation itself, Torah must be contemplated deeply by those who seek to attain its secrets. The outer levels of Torah, the narratives and halakhic readings, are depicted by the Zohar as the "garments" and "body" of Torah. The true self of Torah, however, lies in its soul or kabbalistic mysteries. Even these will eventually give way to a "soul of soul" within the Torah, presumably a place where no distinction exists between the innermost Torah and the divine Self of God.

The notion of primordial Torah, itself derived from ancient images of Wisdom as God's eternal plaything or companion, is a mainstay of rabbinic theology. By the time of the Zohar, this constellation of ideas had evolved into the second of the ten *sefirot*, the "first point" of existence, or the divine mind. All of Torah is contained within it, but in highly

concentrated form. Torah here correspondeds to the letter *yod*, associated with *Ḥokhmah*, and itself but a dot on the page. This is the Torah
that the rabbis had described as written in "black fire on white fire," the
Torah far beyond any ordinary understanding of human language.

The emergence of that secret Wisdom in the form of written Torah
is the great achievement of Moses, hero-prophet of the written Torah
and prototype for the kabbalistic sage as well. Moses has ascended to the
level of *Tif'eret*, that of the blessed Holy One Himself. Only he, of all
humans, is called *ba'ala de-Matronita*, "Husband of the Lady," for he re-
lates to *Shekhinah* as male to female. The written Torah, called "the
Torah of YHVH," thus becomes "the Torah of Moses" as well. The giving of this Torah at Mount Sinai was the unique revelation of God to
humankind. All Israel, including those yet to be born in future generations to the end of time, were present at that revelation and faithfully
agreed to abide by it.

The revelation of Sinai is not yet complete. Moses only began the
process, opening up the wellsprings of divine self-disclosure in the
form of Torah. The various rabbinic teachings and legends that see revelation as ongoing are all part of the Zohar's legacy. Revelation is a
great stream of truth, with more of it revealed in each generation. Here
the Zohar tends to reverse the old bias that favored earlier generations
over those that came after them. The rabbinic dictum that "things that
had not been revealed to Moses were revealed to Rabbi Akiva"[1] is now
transferred to the Zohar's hero, Rabbi Shim'on ben Yoḥai, who is indeed a form of Moses *redivivus*, the bearer of revelation for his own
time. The disciples who receive his teaching constitute a new holy
generation, the likes of which has not existed since that of Sinai and
will not be seen again until the final redemption. Their study of Torah,
and the Zohar's faithful student's contemplation of their insights, carries forward the process of revelation, making it indeed "a great voice
that has never ceased."

1. Midrash Be-Midbar Rabbah 19:6.

12

The Commandments

From its origins, Kabbalah took great interest in the subject of *ta'amei ha-mitsvot*, or the reasons for the commandments. Among the earliest kabbalistic secrets committed to writing were brief hints at the meanings of various commandments, along with mystical explications of prayer and of passages in the prayerbook. This is in no way surprising for a movement that was dedicated, as we have seen, to the defense of rabbinic Judaism in the face of challenges from both philosophy and Christianity. But the frequent and often extended discussion of *mitsvot* in the Zohar requires some further introduction.

The Torah itself offers rather little by way of explanation for the 613 (according to traditional count) commandments that it contains. Occasionally a reward is mentioned in connection with the following of a commandment, as in "so that your days be lengthened," but this is hardly to be taken as the reason for following it. The sacrificial offerings of Leviticus are often described as "sweet savor unto the Lord," perhaps a dim reflection of the prebiblical view that the gods actually partook of and enjoyed the sacrifices. But that view is sharply denied by various passages in the prophetic writings. There are lyrical passages

describing the rewards of a life in harmony with God's commandments, as well as dire warnings to those who transgress them, but the
purpose or meaning of specific commandments is little discussed within
Scripture.

The rabbis understood Israel to have fully accepted the "yoke of the
commandments" at Sinai and viewed the entire Jewish people as committed to the oath of "we shall do and we shall listen" from that time
forward. They even projected the Torah's commandments back onto
the patriarchs, insisting that they had followed every detail of the Law,
even their own rabbinic innovations. Various rabbinic sources insist that
all of the commandments are equally and eternally valid and that no
distinction is to be made among them. "Be as careful regarding a minor
mitsvah as a major one, for you do not know how reward for the commandments is given."[1] If there is a purpose to the commandments it is
singular: to show Israel's devotion to God and to purify Israel through
the disciplined demonstration of that loyalty. "What difference does it
make to the blessed Holy One whether one slaughters an animal from
the neck or from the throat [as prescribed by *halakhah*]? The commandments were given only to purify people."[2]

At the same time, the rabbis did allow for certain categorizations
among the commandments. Best known are two such rubrics. One
distinguishes "commandments between man and God," the devotional and ritual realm, from "commandments between man and his
fellow," the moral-ethical domain. Neither type is taken to be more
vital to the life of holiness than the other, but the distinction between
them is important. This is indicated by the fact that the former category of commandments is preceded by recital of a blessing (since its
essential purpose is that of worship) while the latter is not. Another
pair of categories, overlapping but not identical with these two, is that

1. Mishnah Avot 2:1.
2. Bereshit Rabbah 44:1.

of *ḥuqqim* ("statutes") and *mishpatim* ("judgments"). *Mishpatim* are those commandments that have an obvious value, often an ethical one. Had God not given these commandments, it is sometimes said, humans would have needed to devise them anyway, to allow for the conduct of society. *Ḥuqqim* are divine commandments that defy reason but that must be followed nonetheless. "I have issued a statute, a decree, and you are not permitted to question it [*le-harher aḥareha*]."[3]

A major reason given in the rabbinic sources for following commandments is that of *imitatio dei*, doing that which God does. A famous passage on *devequt*, often quoted in later sources, says that it is impossible to "cleave" to God, whom Scripture describes as "a consuming fire." "Rather cleave to His qualities," is the solution given. "Just as He is merciful and compassionate, so you be merciful and compassionate."[4] This quality of compassion is then illustrated by several divine acts: God visiting the sick (Abraham), God burying the dead (Moses), God celebrating with bride and groom (Adam and Eve), and so on. Thus is one to imitate God in the realm of interpersonal kindness. But some ritual acts are also taken to be in imitation of God: God dons *tefillin*, according to the Talmud; God studies Torah; God observed the first Sabbath; God wrapped Himself in a great prayer shawl, both in Creation and at Sinai.

The medieval philosophers made much use of the earlier categories of commandments, restating *mishpatim* and *ḥuqqim* as "rational" and "disciplinary" commandments. Though formally they were fully committed to both categories, they tried to bring as many commandments as possible into the "rational" camp. This is the purpose of the rather large body of "reasons for the commandments" created by the Jewish rationalists. Maimonides in particular was known for both historical (mostly "countering pagan practices") and educational explanations for the commandments.

3. Midrash Tehillim 9:2.
4. Sotah 14a.

The Kabbalists shared the attempt of other medieval intellectuals to find meaning in the Torah's commandments and in the halakhic praxis that had grown up around them. They understood that the rabbis' simple insistence on unquestioning loyalty to God's Word was not a sufficiently compelling rationale for observance in their day, due to the challenges of other faiths and in the face of the seeming absence of divine reward, as reflected in Israel's exilic and defeated status. But the meaning they sought was of a different order. Observance of the commandments was taken as participation in the divine mystery. Each commandment contained hints as to its origin within the *sefirot* or pointed to a particular combination of forces within the sefirotic world. Knowing these "secrets of the commandments"—handed down first orally, then in writing, by the earliest Kabbalists—allowed one to partake deeply of the *sefirot* themselves. To perform a *mitsvah* with the proper kabbalistic intent (*kavvanah*) was actually to abide in the designated sefirotic realm and to experience the flow of divine energy (*shefa*) that flowed through those *sefirot*. Kabbalistic tradition notes that the word *mitsvah* has its last two letters in common with the name of God (YHVH). The first two letters, *mem* and *tsade*, represent *yod* and *heh* in a widely used reverse alphabet. Thus the word for "commandment" contains within it the name or presence of God, in half-revealed and half-hidden form. To engage in a life of *mitsvot* is to dwell inside that mystery.

The commandments were even more than this. Experiential participation in the sefirotic realm (*devequt*) was only a part of the Kabbalist's intent. He saw the *mitsvot* as divinely given means by which he could actually affect the condition of the inner divine world. The *sefirot* ever needed to be brought together, so that divine life might flow through them and sustain the lower worlds. The powerful forces of evil, as we have seen, are arrayed against this cause. In choosing Israel, God has provided a very powerful and efficacious set of tools by which to combat evil and bring about sefirotic union. This was especially true regarding the *Shekhinah*, who dwelt in a semipermanent state of exile from the upper *sefirot*. "The uniting of the blessed Holy One and His *Shekhinah*" became for the Castilian Kabbalists the overwhelming goal of the religious life, and virtually all of the commandments were viewed as part of this effort.

This understanding of the commandments, referred to as *theurgy* in the scholarly literature on Kabbalah, in fact veers much closer to magic than do other interpretations of Judaism. The belief that human actions can have a direct impact on God, and the sense that God in some way requires or depends on those actions, would have been anathema to the philosophers, and for good reason. It was Naḥmnanides, the great antiphilosophic voice among the early Kabbalists, who claimed (based on certain strands of old rabbinic tradition) that the commandments fulfilled a "divine need." By implication, such a view posits an imperfect Deity and gives real power to humans. What is to prevent humans from misusing the power to fulfill or deny God's "needs" in order to bend the divine will to their own ends? The Zohar is indeed aware of this problem, and is quite careful to distinguish its own theurgic practices from the deeds of magicians, whom it roundly condemns. The Kabbalist is to act only for the sake of the divine unity. He is a faithful devotee of the *Shekhinah*, a knight in Her service. The powerful weapons She has given him are just an extension of the ancient belief that "Israel adds power and strength above." Yes, it is true that the blessings of divine unity will also flow down into this world, even bringing reward to the Kabbalist who has helped to effect that unity. But that is not the intent of the spiritual knight, who knows well "not to be like a servant who ministers to the master for the sake of reward."

There is a list of *mitsvot* in the Zohar, referred to as *Piqqudin*, that begins a detailed accounting of each of the commandments and its sefirotic setting. Unfortunately only a small part of the list exists, and it is not known whether the rest was ever written. Rabbi Moses de Leon wrote a Hebrew work entitled *Sefer ha-Rimmon*, which offers a fuller list of *ta'amey ha-mitsvot*, very much in the spirit of the Zohar. Various individual commandments are interpreted in his other works as well, as in the writings of several contemporaries. The *Ra'aya Meheimna*, printed within the Zohar, also offers a fuller list of the commandments and their kabbalistic meaning, although one supplied by a slightly later author writing in the Zoharic tradition.

Throughout the pages of the Zohar, however, there is frequent discussion of the *mitsvot*. The Zohar is especially partial to certain seemingly mysterious practices such as *tefillin* (phylacteries), *tsitsit* (fringes on the four-cornered garment), *shofar* (blowing of the ram's horn) and *arba'ah minim* (the "four species" of the Sukkot ritual). The multiple aspect of each of these practices refers to various *sefirot*, especially the fourfold groupings of *Tif'eret* and *Malkhut*, with one or another pairing from the right and left sides of the sefirotic chart (*Hokhmah/Binah, Hesed/Gevurah,* or *Netsah/Hod*, depending on the *mitsvah* and the particular passage). These secrets are described in elaborate detail and must be seen as contemplative exercises that were meant to accompany and enhance the actual performance of the rites involved. There is a very strong sense of sacramental piety about the Zohar, with the commandments leading their doer into a realm of infinite and mysterious inner sanctity.

In this context, the sacred calendar of Israel takes on special importance, and both Sabbath and festivals are given great significance. Some of the most beautifully lyrical passages in the Zohar describe the Sabbath, the time of *hieros gamos*, or the sacred marriage between *Shekhinah* and Her Spouse. These writings inspired later Kabbalists to create a special ritual for the greeting of the Sabbath Bride, probably the best-known and most widely accepted kabbalistic innovation to Jewish practice. The ritual of the Day of Atonement is also described at length in the Zohar as a time when *Ḥesed* triumphs in expiation of Israel's sins, defeating the power of *Din* or judgment and uplifting the *Shekhinah*. Passover celebrates the redemption from Egypt that is the appearance of *Binah*, the undiminished redeeming presence that rescues both Israel and *Shekhinah* from the House of Bondage. The presence of *Binah* also leads to the counting of fifty days until *Shavu'ot*, a holiday of both *Binah* (jubilee, the fiftieth day) and *Tif'eret* (the written Torah). The Zohar also acclaims a supposedly ancient practice, mentioned for the first time in its pages, of staying awake through *Shavu'ot* night to study Torah and await the renewal of revelation at dawn. This practice too, although possibly an adaptation of Easter and Pentacost vigils that were well known in the medieval church, came to be widely observed by later generations.

The sacramental character of the Zohar's understanding of the commandments naturally leads it to have a greater interest in the "between man and God" realm than in the ethical-moral category of *mitsvot*. But this is not entirely the case. The Zohar is quite concerned with charity and proper treatment of the poor. The giving of alms is interpreted in precisely the same sort of sacramental way as are "ritual" commandments, as an extending of the hand to the ever-needy and "poor" *Shekhinah*. Such ritualized readings are found with regard to other seemingly "rational" commandments as well, bearing witness to an attempt by the Kabbalists to undermine the philosophers' distinction and view all of the commandments as belonging to a single sacral realm.

Such a unitive view is important to the Zohar because it sees the *mitsvot* as "limbs of the King," or aspects of a single sacred structure. While the tenfold grid of sefirotic symbols is always central to its imagination, the notion of 613 commandments, divided into 248 injunctions and 365 prohibitions (supposedly parallel to 248 "limbs" and 365 "sinews" of the human body), is also the object of a good deal of speculation, including numerological associations, in the Zohar and throughout Kabbalah. The commandments are an organic whole. To observe them is to build up the "form of the Shekhinah" and at the same time to acquire for one's own soul a proper "garment" that will be required for passage into the world to come.

Because the Zohar is such a vast compendium of Jewish lore, it also reflects in significant ways on actual details of Jewish practice as carried out by the circle of Kabbalists who created it. While these Jews were clearly native to Castile and therefore followers of the Sephardic liturgical rite, it is interesting to note that there is a good deal of Franco-German influence on certain practices within the Zohar. The esoteric secrets that were imported to Spain from Provencal circles, themselves linked to groups further north, seem to have brought with them some typically Ashkenazic practices and attitudes as well. While these are witnessed in certain fine details of halakhic praxis, they may also be present in the Zohar's attitude toward the commandments as a whole. The strong emphasis on theurgy, as well as an openness to the real efficacy of magic (even while opposing its use), is more reflective of the Ashkenazic setting than of Spain, where rationalistic influence, left over from centuries of Islamic domination, was somewhat stronger. It could be said that the mystical-pietistic circles out of which the Zohar emerged represented a new amalgamation of some of the strongest elements in the Sephardic and Ashkenazic traditions.

13

Avodah:
The Life of Worship

Among the commandments of the Torah, the Zohar pays special attention to Judaism's key acts of worship, the sacrificial rites of the ancient Temple, and prayer, the "service of the heart," which replaced sacrifice after the Temple's destruction, more than a millennium before the Zohar was written. As a work focused on the devotional life, the Zohar, it may be said, views all the commandments as forms of *avodah*, or worship. Nevertheless, the frequent and often lengthy treatments given to the services of both Temple and synagogue require discussion in their own right.

The aggadic tradition in fact contains two views of the relationship between liturgical prayer and sacrifice. One view indeed claims that the fixed prayers of the synagogue came about in lieu of the sacrifices. In particular, the required daily morning and afternoon *amidah* prayers replaced the regular communal offerings (*tamid*) of dawn and dusk each day. The other view claims, on the basis of a reading of various biblical verses, that prayer itself is ancient, each of the three daily services having been initiated by one of the patriarchs,. While the former view is much closer to historical accuracy (though not completely, since pro-torabbinic prayer already existed in late Second Temple times), the latter makes a metahistoric claim, seeing it as unthinkable that there could be any sort of Judaism without regularly defined forms of prayer. The very sacrifice offered by Abraham, that of his son Isaac on Mount Moriah, site of the future Temple, is here preceded by Abraham's morning prayer, offered on the dawn when he set forth on that fateful journey. The demand for human sacrifice is forever negated by this story; animal slaughter takes its place. But fixed prayer, says this *aggadah*, remains an unbroken tradition since Abraham.

Rabbinic Judaism, created largely in response to the catastrophe of Jerusalem's destruction, preserved a great loyalty to the memory of Temple, priest, and sacrificial altar. In contrast to Christianity, it did not accept that the Temple worship had been set aside by a new dispensation of divine grace. The razing of the Temple was the deed of the wicked Romans, and the rabbis would continue to wrestle with its theological meaning for centuries to come. Meanwhile, the Mishnah codified the laws of sacrifice and ritual purity as though the Temple were still standing, indicating an early hope that it would be rebuilt, just as the Second Temple had replaced that destroyed by the Babylonians some six centuries earlier. The midrashic glorification of both Moses' Tabernacle and Solomon's Temple (especially at the moments of their dedication) also points in this direction.

For the present, however, the Temple cult, or *avodah*, had been suspended and replaced by prayer, *avodah sheba-lev* ("the service in the heart"), and this was by no means to be taken lightly. The daily *amidot* (two required plus one voluntary) and recitations of the *shema* ("Hear O Israel"—Deuteronomy 6:4 and so on—twice each day) were codified and discussed extensively by the early sages. Prayer was understood to have great power both in the life of the individual and in the collective life of Israel. According to a well-known aggadic motif, the daily prayers of Israel were collected by angelic emissaries and placed as a crown upon God's head, much as the rings of smoke rising from the altar had once reached heaven, offering an aroma that aroused divine pleasure and bringing blessing to the world. This mythical assimilation of liturgical prayer into the role and powers of Temple sacrifice took place in the generations immediately following the great destruction. It was centered around the ritual proclamation of the two key phrases of prophetic vision: "Holy, holy, holy is the Lord of Hosts; the whole earth is filled with His glory" (Is. 6:3) and "Blessed be the glory of God from His place" (Ez. 3:12). These are both called out at once by God's angelic and human hosts in the very moment that the prayers arise and are received in heaven. The fact that the ritual proclamation of these words exists in Christianity as well as in Judaism stands as testimony to the first-century origins and mystical setting of this *qedushah* rite.

Certain mixed feelings, however, regarding the sacrificial cult were contained within the vast and often complex rabbinic corpus. While everyone joined in mourning and bewailing the destruction, some remembered as well how corrupt the Jerusalem Temple had been in its later years, from the Pharisaic or protorabbinic viewpoint. Perhaps it was these memories that led some midrashic voices to depict the building of Moses' Tabernacle, following the incident of the Golden Calf, as a response to the obviously idolatrous tendencies of the ancient Israelites. When God sought to destroy His sinful people, Moses cried out to God (as the Midrash has it)[1] that He was in fact responsible for their sins: "The excess of gold and silver that You gave them (from the plunder of the Egyptians) caused them to build the idol!" A parable describes Israel as the son of a rich man who is given a full purse by his father, who then seats him at the entrance to a house of ill repute. Is the

1. Berakhot 32a.

poor lad to be blamed for the ensuing whoredom, or is it the father who led him into temptation? It is hard to read this Midrash and not think of the Greek idols that reputedly stood in the late Second Temple precincts, supported by a Hellenized priesthood seduced by rich purses of gold and silver. It was the corrupting influence of wealth, so the Midrash claims, that led those descendents of Aaron to accept idolatry in God's house. Some among the rabbis went so far as to proclaim that all the commandments regarding the Tabernacle and the sacrificial system had come about only as a result of Israel's attraction to idolatry. By implication this would seem to mean that the revelation in its original intent might have preferred another form of worship, perhaps that of the heart rather than the sacrificial altar.

While such conclusions remain vague and implicit in the rabbinic sources, their implications are spelled out quite clearly in the writings of medieval thinkers. Rabbi Bahya Ibn Paquda (late eleventh century), one of the great spiritualizers of Judaism in the Middle Ages, shows a clear preference for the "Duties of the Heart" (the title of his work) over those of the limbs, and clearly understands worship as belonging in its essence to the former category. Maimonides follows him in proclaiming the Torah's prescription of sacrificial worship as a compromise with the weak nature of the Exodus generation, made up of slaves whose ancestors had lived for generations in ancient Egypt, the very heart of idolatry. While his code follows the Mishnah in including sacrificial laws and laws of Temple purity, Maimonides' philosophic writing clearly expresses his preference for prayer over animal slaughter as a way of coming into God's presence.

In contrast to these philosophical views, the Zohar devotes an extraordinary amount of attention to the Temple cult, to the priesthood, and to all aspects of the Torah that are associated with them. It is in the course of these discussions, in fact, that the view of the commandments as "divine need" becomes most apparent. Here the Zohar builds on aggadic traditions that came surprisingly close to understanding sacrifice as a way of "feeding" or strengthening God. Throughout its treatment of the Temple cult, the Zohar clearly identifies fully the two types of worship, sacrifice and prayer, with one another. It is not unusual for both types to be discussed in a single passage in which the Zohar leaps back and forth between the synagogue and Temple rites. The Zohar makes powerful, even audacious, claims for the power of kabbalistic prayer and devotion to unify the *sefirot* and bring about the flow of divine blessing. It may be that its authors were aware of the dangers of such claims—those of a theurgy that verges on magic. It may also be that they were concerned with the reception these claims might find among Spanish Jews still imbued with the spirit of philosophy, who would have scoffed at the assertion of so much human power in the act of prayer. It was thus "safer" to couch the most extreme of kabbalistic claims for worship's power in expressions of devotion to the ancient Temple cult, one that in any case had not been practiced in a thousand years. The initiate reader would well understand that "prayer was instituted parallel to the regular offerings," and thus all that was being said of the Temple altar's powers was true of the heart's inner altar as well.

The Temple, along with all that took place within it, is viewed by the Zohar as an object of contemplation and a paradigm of inner spiritual experience. Its courtyards and chambers, culminating in the innermost Holy of Holies, are parallel to both cosmic hierarchies and stages of human devotion. The Temple's appurtenances, from the basin used for priestly washing to the great Menorah itself, are all objects of symbolic interpretation. In this the Zohar builds on the earlier Kabbalah and stands parallel as well to the contemporary German Hasidic tradition, both of which turned back to these classic forms, linking them frequently to the experience of liturgical prayer. Similarly (as we shall see in the next section), the Kabbalist or *tzaddik* stood in place of the priest, and all the powers attributed to one referred by implication to the other as well. But all this, spoken in the context of the ancient Temple, was said in a way that would not offend, remaining semihidden from those who did not know how to properly unpack the Zohar's secrets.

Among the lengthiest sections in the Zohar are its homilies on the latter portions of Exodus, where the construction of the Tabernacle is set forth in great detail. The Tabernacle and all that it contained are often taken to represent the mysteries of *Binah* and *Malkhut*, which are sometimes designated as "upper" and "lower" Tabernacle or even as "First" and "Second" Temple. The Tabernacle is described as a microcosm both of the terrestrial world and of the worlds above. The Kabbalist, serving as a priest at the inner altar, stands parallel to the angel Michael, who is the high priest in the Temple of *Malkhut*, and even to the blessed Holy One Himself, who serves that role in the highest Temple of *Binah*. These discussions are interwoven with the Zohar's commentary on the liturgy, reflecting the links between sacrificial and verbal forms of devotional life. The section *Terumah* in particular contains a large fragment of an ordered commentary on the synagogue service.

Despite the seeming "naturalness" of locating its treatment of sacramental piety in those Torah passages that command and then describe the erection of the wilderness Tabernacle, the Zohar in fact makes clear its preference for the grand Temple of Solomon over the portable sanctuary of Moses. While not disputing Moses' status as the greatest of all prophets, the Zohar's authors see Solomon as the mystical hierophant par excellence, the human being who attained the greatest success in unifying the *sefirot* in a long-lasting way and thus bringing divine blessing to flow through all the worlds. Solomon, it is important to remember, symbolically represents *Yesod* on the sefirotic chart. He or it is the agent through which *Malkhut* is linked to the divine forces above.

The purpose of the sacrifices offered in both Tabernacle and Temple was the bringing together of those cosmic forces. The Kabbalists repeat tirelessly Sefer Bahir's assertion that sacrifice is called *qorban* in Hebrew ("offering," related to *Q-R-B*, "to approach," "to be near") because it draws the inner divine forces near to one another. The various sacrifices of the Torah's priestly code fulfill different aspects of this unification: the reconciliation of left and right (usually including the subjegation of left to the greater power of the right side's love), the linking of *Binah* with the *sefirot* below her, or the ever-dominant union of male and female, the center of contemplative unification for the Zohar. Crucial to the fulfillment of the Temple cult's true purpose was the priest's awareness of the kabbalistic intentions of his deeds. As one reads the Zoharic descriptions of the priest, either when he turns toward God to offer expiation of Israel's sins or when he blesses the people with shining face, it becomes clear that he is the prototype of the Kabbalist himself, one whose knowledge of worship's secrets gives infinite power and meaning to his own acts of devotion, now in the forms of liturgical prayers.

But there may as well be another reason for the Zohar's fascination with the Temple rites and the close linkage of sacrifice and prayer. The elaborate descriptions of the Temple service and the attribution of great mystery to them offer the reader a Jewish alternative, albeit a fantastic one, to the pomp and ceremony of the medieval Catholic Church. The decades after the Reconquista, as we have noted, were marked by the erection of great cathedrals in Castile, as throughout the Iberian peninsula. These were vast structures within which, especially as they were filled with solemn music and the aroma of incense, the worshiper was to feel a palpable sense of sacred presence. Partly because of legal restrictions, but also because of differences in tradition, we have no evidence that Castilian synagogues in any way rivaled these structures. In Christianity, unlike in Judaism, the cathedral had fully replaced the ancient Temple as a locus of sacred space. The synagogue, even formally designated as *miqdash me'at* ("a lesser sanctuary"), was seen as a mere temporary stand-in for the one Temple, hopefully soon to be rebuilt.

The Zohar, anxious to counter whatever attraction Jews might have to the beauty and mystery of those great churches, takes pains to ascribe endless glory to God's single true dwelling upon earth, the Temple of the great King Solomon. This Temple was a this-worldly house of God, parallel to God's true "House," the *Shekhinah*. She is the heavenly Jerusalem, the holy Tabernacle, House, Palace, the place the great King enters and makes His home. Moses' entry into the earthly Tabernacle and Solomon's moment of dedicting the Temple were earthly imitations of God's entry into *Shekhinah* (or the union of *Tif'eret* and *Malkhut*), the sacred marriage that stands at the center of the Zohar's spiritual life. This is *raza de-razin*, the *secret secretorum* that surpasses all others, calling forth the loyalty of Jews to a *mysterium* greater than that offered on the altar of any church.

This reason for paying such great attention to the Temple cult applies especially to the priesthood and to the power of blessing that lay in the hands of Aaron and his descendents. Unlike their brethren who lived in Islamic societies, Castilian Jews dwelled in the shadow of a powerful and active priesthood, one that made full use of the quasi-magical powers of priestly blessing. The Christian priest's hands and mouth, which conveyed the sacraments and spoke the words of transformation that made them real, also had the power to heal the sick, to fructify the fields, and to protect one from enemies. While Catholic theology understood that these were the blessings of God, conferred through the priest as His humble agent, in the eyes of the people the priest clearly had a part in these powers and was feared and respected accordingly. The medieval rabbinate by tradition bore almost nothing of this *mysterium*. The Zohar's authors, perceiving its attractiveness and importance, commented frequently and powerfully on the priestly blessing, on the divine presence of the *sefirot* that enters the priests' hands, and on the power of such blessing both to affect the upper unity and to bring forth the flow of divine bounty. Once more the

message was that the Israelites had the *real* cult, priesthood, and connection to the Holy. Even if historical circumstance had brought Israel
low and seemed to show favor to the religion of its foes, Jews were to
remain true to the now partially revealed secret faith of Aaron and his
sons, and to receive blessing from their descendents, who still bore the
ancient right to bless Israel in the name of God, to "place My name
upon them, that I bless them" (Num. 6:27).

As a work reflecting on and seeking to defend traditional forms of
Jewish practice, the Zohar does not limit its discussions of prayer to the
sort of rarified calls for inwardness and concentration that characterized such treatises as Bahya's *Duties of the Heart*. The Zohar is interested
in the forms of Jewish prayer practiced in its day. It speaks avidly in favor of communal worship and advocates great respect for the synagogue and the public prayers recited within it. Reflections abound on
the structure of the service, especially on the *shema*, the *amidah*, and the
supplications (*tahanun*) that follow it in the weekday service. The public reading of the Torah is treated as a grand event, one reverberating
with echoes of Israel's standing before Sinai when the Torah was first
given. The special prayers of the Sabbath liturgy are also seen by the
Zohar as grand testimony to that day's holy status as parallel to *Malkhut*
(the seventh of the lower *sefirot*) in the realm of time.

In order to demonstrate the complex and multileveled treatment of
both commandment and liturgy in the Zohar, we might do well to review its discussion of a single *mitsvah*, that of reciting the *shema*. This
twice-daily obligation, implied already by the biblical text (Deut. 6:7),
is fully codified in the Mishnah and is universally accepted as a corner-
stone of Jewish religious practice. The power of the *shema*'s opening
line ("Hear O Israel, YHVH our God, YHVH is One") as a declara-
tion of Judaism's monotheistic faith and the association of the *shema*
with Jewry's history of martyrdom both lent even greater drama and
importance to the fulfillment of this commandment. The Zohar dis-

cusses the *shema* in several key passages,[2] each emphasizing one or more aspects of this practice's secret meaning. The 248 words that constitute the full text of the *shema* represent the 248 limbs of the human body; by reciting these holy words one brings holiness to each of one's limbs and causes divine energy to flow into it. The twenty-five letters of the opening line and the 24 in the doxology that follows it ("Blessed be the name of His glorious kingdom forever!") together represent the forty-nine gates of *Binah*, or the seven lower *sefirot*, each containing all the others, in the fullness of their source. The six words of the *shema's* opening proclamation stand for the six lower *sefirot*, constituting an "upper unity" parallel to *Malkhut*, the "lower unity" represented by the doxology. The recitation of the *shema* is the joining of these two levels of inner divine oneness. The fact that two letters of the *shema*, the *ayin* (the letter *ayin* also represents the number seventy) of *shema* and the *dalet* of *ehad*, are written in large script in the Torah scroll indicates that all seventy names of God, themselves an expansion of the seven lower *sefirot*, are conjoined in *Malkhut*, represented by the *dalet*.

Among the many *kavvanot* of the *shema*, however, the Zohar is most interested in the sequence of three divine names (*YHVH Elohenu YHVH*) that occurs in the opening verse. Some Zohar passages inter pret these names as referring to *Hesed*, *Gevurah*, and *Tif'eret*, the central triad of the divine persona. Elsewhere the three names are seen as extending across the entire sefirotic world, representing *Hokhmah*, *Tif'eret*, and *Malkhut*. The domininant tradition, however, is that the three stand for *Hokhmah*, *Binah*, and *Tif'eret*, the two hidden sources (or "parents") of the personified Deity and the divine figure itself. The six words of the *shema* then extend *Tif'eret* in all directions, encompassing the entire divine realm. *Malkhut* is represented by the concluding *dalet* of the word *ehad*, traditionally elongated in performance. *Malkhut* is both here and elsewhere associated with the letter *dalet* because *dal* means "poor," and

2. 1:12a; 2:133b–134b, 160b, 216b; 3:236b, 258a, 263a.

Malkhut, as the receptive principle, seemingly has no blessing of her own until she receives that which is poured into her from beyond.

These three names of God are also those that are traditionally used on the outside of the mezuzah scroll affixed to the doorposts of Jewish homes. There the three names are written in hidden fashion, each letter replaced by the one following it in the alphabet (rendering *YHVH Elohenu YHVH* as *Kuzu Bmukhsz Kuzu*). The sequence is supposed to possess a mysterious apotropaic, or protective, strength as a writing out of God's "full" name in all its awesome power. This custom, mentioned in the early fourteenth century *Arba'ah Turim* of Jacob ben Asher, may have originated among the Rhineland *Ḥasidim.* It is likely that the Zohar, influenced by similar traditions, views the pronunciation of these three names in the *shema* as an especially forceful invocation of divine presence and power.

The tripartite character of this most essential Jewish calling upon God's name did not go unnoticed by later Christian students of Kabbalah, who hoped to see in it a secret reference to their own Trinitarian views. While there is of course no basis for such a reading of the Zohar, it is possible that here too the Kabbalists were responding to a well-known structure of the dominant religious tradition. In that case we would understand the Zoharic authors as seeking to point to the "true" trinity, a series of three levels within the sefirotic realm. These would probably be the most hidden (the first triad of *sefirot*), the divine Person (centered around *Tif'eret*), and the immanent divine Presence (*Shekhinah* or *Malkhut*). Elsewhere the Zohar refers to these three levels of divinity by use of the three pronouns He, Thou, and I.[3] Thus the recitation of the *shema* is seen as truly encompassing *yiḥud ha-shem,* the proclamation of God's oneness across all dimensions of existence.

3. 1:65b, 204a–b; 2:90a; 3:290a. The hidden Godhead is "He" because the Hebrew grammatical term for the "third person" is *nistar,* literally, "the hidden one." This aspect of the Deity can be spoken of, but not addressed.

14

The *Tsaddiq*
and the Life of Piety

The human ideal of classic Jewish piety is described in the old rabbinic sources by several terms. He (the ideal is always male) is a *talmid hakham*, a "disciple of the wise"; a *hasid*, or pious lover of God; and a *tsaddiq*, or righteous one. The precise meaning of these terms and the interplay between them has been discussed considerably both within the sources and by scholars attempting to understand and categorize the value structure of rabbinic Judaism, so lacking in systematic presentation of its basic assumptions. *Talmid hakham* refers primarily to the world of Talmudic learning and is the designation by which the rabbis most commonly described themselves. *Hasid* generally bespeaks an extreme pietistic ideal, referring to one who goes beyond the letter of the Law in a display of selfless devotion. Some texts show an edge of tension between the *talmid hakham* and the *hasid*. The ideal of the former incorporates a degree of sobriety and communal responsibility, while the latter seeks to cast all reservation to the wind in offering his soul in each moment on the altar of devotion to God.

The third term, *tsaddiq*, presents a somewhat more complicated picture. It is used in the forensic sense to refer to one who is "innocent," or righteous as opposed to sinful. At times this seems to include all those whose merits outweigh their faults on the scales of divine justice—hopefully, a healthy percentage of the population. Some texts further distinguish between the complete *tsaddiq*, one who has routed the evil urge altogether, and the incomplete *tsaddiq*, one who still struggles, even if successfully, with the temptations of the flesh. But the word *tsaddiq* is also used in a more limited sense to refer to a special class of spiritual supermen, those who sustain the world by their merit. "*Tsaddiq* is the foundation of the world," says Scripture (Prov. 10:25),[1] and the rabbis add, perhaps borrowing from the Hellenistic picture of Atlas, "The world stands upon a single pillar. Who is that? The *tsaddiq*."[2] Rabbi Shim'on ben Yoḥai referred to himself, according to a well-known *aggadah*,[3] as the single righteous one of his generation, perhaps giving birth to the coinage *tsaddiq ha-dor*, "the righteous one of the generation."

As distinct genres of moralistic and mystical literature began to develop in eleventh- and twelfth-century Europe, the terms *ḥasid* and *tsaddiq* took on new importance. *Ḥakham* or *talmid ḥakham* was generally left alone as the designation of scholars in the ongoing field of Talmudic-halakhic learning. But in such diverse circles as those represented by Baḥya Ibn Paquda's *Duties of the Heart* (written in eleventh-century Muslim Spain, showing considerable Sufi influence) and Judah he-Ḥasid's *Book of the Pious* (written in twelfth-century Rhineland), *ḥasid* was used to characterize the ideal pious type. This was also true in the earliest circle of Kabbalists, where Rabbi Isaac the Blind was generally referred to simply as "the *ḥasid*," following traditions borne by his distinguished Provencal family.

The Zohar, however, overwhelmingly prefers *tsaddiq* to *ḥasid* in rep-

1. The literal meaning is probably "The righteous one stands firm forever."
2. Hagigah 12b.
3. Bereshit Rabbah 35:2.

resenting its ideal. *Hasid* is philologically related to *Hesed* and is thence assocated with Abraham, who did all for the love of God. This figure does appear occasionally in the Zohar's pages. But the mythmaking imagination is much more interested in the *tsaddiq*, the earthly incarnation of the ninth *sefirah*, *Yesod* or "foundation," whose very name derives from this association with the *tsaddiq*, based on the verse from Proverbs cited above. The "pillar" on which the world stands represents the phallic form we discussed earlier in connection with the ninth *sefirah*. This linkage is underscored by the fact that in the Zohar's Aramaic the word *qeyama* means both "pillar" and "covenant," referring to the covenant of circumcision or the circumcised phallus itself. But the same pillar also functions as what scholars of religion call the *axis mundi*, a central pole of existence that links upper and lower worlds. *Tsaddiq*, both divine and human, is the personification of this *qeyama*, joining together heaven and earth in a union that can be understood in both mythic-cosmological and moral-covenantal terms.

As pillar or channel linking the upper and lower worlds, the *tsaddiq* is a great source of blessing. Rabbi Shim'on and other figures in the Zohar often take on that priestly role, conveying the light of God's presence to the company around them. The common designation of Rabbi Shim'on as *botsina qaddisha*, "the holy lamp," is a reflection of this function. While the *tsaddiqim* are very much elite figures, there is also a tendency within the Zohar for them to share the qualities of *tsaddiq* as broadly as possible, bringing all of Israel into their fold. Among the biblical verses most frequently quoted by the Zohar is "Your people are all righteous (*tsaddiqim*); they will forever inherit the land . . ." (Is. 60:21). This verse is used in defense of Israel, which is very much a part of the Zohar's agenda. (The "land" here is taken to refer to *Shekhinah*, ever in Israel's midst.) Its authors saw themselves as leaders of the beleagured people, standing in the tradition of the prophets and the early rabbis. This role of leadership included reproof of Israel for their sins, sometimes in the strongest terms. But it also included defending them before the punishing arm of heaven, trying to protect them from excesses of divine wrath. The righteous stand poised between heaven and earth, seeking to defend their people both from the wiles of *sitra ahara*, ever seeking to lead them astray, and from the destruction that will be the result of their sins. The *tsaddiq* as prophet-leader also comes to console Israel, the same people he has so harshly reproved, assuring them that God will never wholly depart from them.

In designating its heroes with the mantle of *tsaddiq*, the Zoharic authors were by no means abandoning the ideal of Torah study as their central religious preoccupation. Although in its Talmudic designation *tsaddiq* seems quite separate from the ideal of learning, the Zohar sees the "righteous" and "those who occupy themselves with Torah" as one and the same. Of course for the Zohar this refers to kabbalistic study and interpretation of the Torah in terms of the *sefirot*. The righteous are those who engage in such study, by which they partake of the divine *tsaddiq*'s task of upholding the universe. The world exists "for the sake of Torah" and "for the sake of the righteous." In the consciousness of the Zohar, these are one and the same. Thus the "companions" or disciples of Rabbi Shim'on, the ideal type of *tsaddiq* in the Zohar, are seen primarily in the role of loving students and interpreters of Torah.

We have mentioned previously the combination of sexual energy and commitment to chastity that constitutes the symbol cluster of *Yesod*. The same is true of the earthly *tsaddiq*, as personified both by Rabbi Shim'on and by tales of other righteous figures scattered throughout the Zohar. The *tsaddiq* is the potent bearer of righteous souls into this world, and his life is fulfilled only by marriage and fatherhood. He is potent also with regard to the worlds above; the energy of his love-driven prayers arouse the *Shekhinah* and thence course through the sefirotic realm. But he achieves this power only by going in the way of Joseph the Righteous, conquering temptation and living in accord with the strictest interpretation of Judaism's sexual taboos. The Zohar is fiercely concerned with the sins of onanism, physical contact with one's wife before her postmenstrual ablution, and sexual relations with non-Jewish women. The vain spilling of seed, so laden with symbolic meaning in the kabbalistic imagination, is condemned as being a sin worse than murder. Such seed is gathered up by Lilith or Na'amah and used to give birth to demons. Onanism is even designated by the Zohar as the one sin for which there is no atonement through the power of repentance

The sin of sexual relations between men receives little mention in the Zohar and does not seem to have been a special concern. Yet it is fair to say that a strong current of homoerotic energy is found within its pages. The open displays of affection between master and disciples, including kisses on the lips, the exclamations of love and devotion to one another, and the intense portrayals of male bonding and companionship that abound in the text all point in this direction. It was perhaps partly for this reason that the Zohar needed to insist on marriage and procreation as essential to the life of the companions. But we are left with a somewhat unsettling picture of a group of men sharing an intensely erotic (and apparently heterosexual) life of sacred fantasy while declaring their passionate affection for one another, sometimes expressed in the language of the Song of Songs. Recent scholarship, particularly the work of Elliot Wolfson, has begun to question the balance between heteroerotic and homoerotic elements in the Zohar's worldview, especially around the relationship between *Yesod* and *Malkhut*. While *Malkhut* as *Shekhinah* is bride and female partner of *Yesod*, she is also described as *atarah*. *Atarah* means "crown," but the term is also used to describe the corona of the circumcised phallus. If the relationship of the final two *sefirot* is partly that of phallus and corona, we have a picture of purely self-oriented male sexual fantasy, hidden behind the brightly described pictures of male-female union. Here the female could be seen more as to be incorporated within the male than as truly encountered as other. This tendency within Zohar scholarship, obviously influenced by trends within contemporary feminist thought, remains somewhat controversial.

The strong sexual component in Zoharic symbolism surely had much to do with the work's powerful impact and long-lasting hold on the Jewish religious imagination. This is especially true regarding the repressive or ascetic elements within the Zohar. The kabbalistic ethos that developed in the sixteenth and seventeenth centuries represents the most extreme position ever articulated within Judaism on the dangers, both to soul and cosmos, of even the faintest degree of sexual pollution. The various works known as *Tiqqunei Teshuvah*, or Orders of Penitence, prescribe extraordinary regimens of fasting and self-punishment even for thoughts of sin or involuntary emissions of semen. The Zohar was used to create an atmosphere that was alive with fear of contact with menstrual blood or with women who were not properly purified. This attitude was extended, both within the Zohar's pages and in the society later created in its wake, to an actual fear of women as sorceresses and as bearers of demonic energy. This negative view of women remains a leitmotif that exists side by side with the lavish and affectionate portrayals of *Shekhinah* as the bride arrayed among her maidens, their light and beauty extending throughout the worlds.

15

The Jewish People,
Exile, and Messiah

The Zohar is not only a book of Jewish teachings and Jewish symbols,
a commentary on the Torah. It is also a book of the Jewish people.
The shared historical situation of Jewry, contained primarily within
the drama of ancient glory, destruction, exile, and dream of restoration, is very much that of the Zohar as well. In adapting itself to the
midrashic form, the Zohar returns to themes that had already rever-
berated through Jewish preaching for nearly a thousand years.

One of these themes is the mourning for Jerusalem's destruction and
the loss of the Temple cult. The destruction of the Temple is vividly felt
in the Zohar, where so much loving attention is lavished on biblical
verses dealing with sacrifices, incense offerings, and other aspects of the
ancient shrine. In choosing to deliver its message through the mouths
of Rabbi Shim'on ben Yoḥai and his disciples, who lived less than a
century after the great destruction, the Zohar opted for a vision of Judaism in which the memory and pain of that trauma were fresh and
undiminished. It succeeds in conveying the immediate sense of loss, and
with it capturing, to a remarkable degree, how alive that feeling still was
even a millennium later. This is true especially of the poignant little

treatise called Zohar to Lamentations,[1] contained within *Zohar Hadash*, but also in the many references to the theme of destruction and its lamentation throughout the work.

The exile of Israel sets a tone that is felt throughout the Zohar. It serves as a dark and tragic counterpoint to the lush colors of eros described earlier. Master and disciples represent homeless Israel, encountering wise teachers and mysterious holy men in the course of what seem to be endless and aimless wanderings. Their exile parallels that of Israel, as we have indicated. But Israel's own exile is itself a replication of the universal predicament, since all humans share in the exile from Eden resulting from Adam's sin. All souls (there is some confusion as to whether they are "the souls of Israel" or of all humanity) were there in Adam, as they will be present in the Messiah. The Zohar bears a strong sense that humankind, and the universe with it, exists in a fallen state. *Shekhinah*, long said by the rabbis to participate in the exile and tribulations of Israel, is portrayed in the Zohar as victim of Adam's sin and of all of human transgression that comes in its wake. The longing for redemption that so much pervades the classical Jewish imagination is transformed in the Zohar, where it is depicted as the longing of God and cosmos alongside that of the suffering people. All of them long to be redeemed.

Given that strong sense of history, one might expect that the Zohar would be a highly messianic work, filled with the sense of impending redemption. That indeed is the character of certain works of Kabbalah, including some contemporaneous with the Zohar, and many that have come in its wake. The fact is, however, that messianism plays a relatively minor role in the main body of the Zohar. The Kabbalists who fill its pages have learned to invoke the presence of God within the life of Ju-

1. Available in an English translation by Seth Brody in Rabbi Ezra ben Solomon of Gerona, *Commentary on the Song of Songs and Other Kabbalistic Commentaries* (Kalamazoo: Western Michigan University, 1999).

daism, enriching both prayer and commandments, as we have seen, by use of their powerful symbolic language. The *kavvanah*, or mystical intention, of the Kabbalist does affect the upper universe, bringing the *sefirot* into harmony with one another. But it seems to do so only in a temporary way. The forces of evil are great, and this world has a natural predisposition to fall under their spell.

The Zohar seems to accept this reality and its heroes do not openly rebel against it. Human efforts toward the restoration of the *Shekhinah* operate within the framework of certain rhythms, both historical and liturgical. The regularity of ritual patterns, especially those of Sabbath and weekday, is well known. But even the "historical" fluctuations of *Shekhinah's* fate seem to be reframed into what is primarily a liturgical mode, through the cycle of weekly Torah readings and their homiletical exposition. Thus the exegesis of such potentionally redemption-inspiring events as the erection of the Tabernacle or the sending of spies into the Land of Israel come to stand, as they do in classical Midrash, as part of the well-known annual cycle and do not inspire calls for messianic activism that would break out of that cycle.

Like all general characterizations of the Zohar, this one too should not be taken as absolute. There are some apocalyptic passages within the text, including even hints at dates of the Messiah's arrival. But these are to be expected in a work of thirteenth-century Jewish preaching, part of the discourse of the age. Our remarks concern the overall tone of the Zohar and are not to be taken as a full accounting of all that is to be found within its pages. The Zohar is indeed concerned with the work of restoration and the Kabbalist is to engage in it constantly. But little hope is held out that this will bring about the end of history or the full redemption that remains the ultimate dream, for the Zohar as for every Jew in its era.

This situation changes dramatically when we turn away from the main Zohar narrative and focus on the two special sections known as the Greater and Lesser Assembly, *Idra Rabba* and *Idra Zuta* (or *Idrot*).[2] Here both the literary style and the symbolic content are quite different from the rest of the Zohar. These are passages that culminate in high drama: the *Idra Rabba* tells of the ecstatic deaths of three of the disciples and the *Idra Zuta* reaches a climax of emotion with Rabbi Shim'on's passing and the devastation that the surviving disciples feel in a world bereft of him. The *Idra Zuta* seems to have been composed as a dramatic conclusion to the Zohar. It is clear that in the *Idrot* the Zohar's central hero has made a transition from the archetype of *tsaddiq* to something very like a messianic or protomessianic figure.

As the ultimate revelation in the lifetime of Rabbi Shim'on, the *Idrot* purport to offer a higher or deeper truth than that found elsewhere in the Zohar. This truth may correspond to the "soul of soul" level of interpreting the Torah, one that the Zohar has told us will be revealed only in messianic times. Now that veil is pulled aside, as it were, and the Zohar lets the reader in on this most profound level of discourse. The teachings revealed here supposedly come directly from *Keter*, the highest and most purely compassionate rung within the sefirotic world.

The new Kabbalah of the *Idrot* constitutes the most radically anthropomorphic section of the Zohar. The by-now conventional symbolic language of the ten *sefirot* is set aside in favor of a new five-part configuration of the Godhead. These five figures are designated as *partsufim*, or "countenances," meaning that each is a face of God and a way God looks at the world. In the place of *Keter*, the mysterious source of the *sefirot*, is the face of God as a loving elder. Sometimes this countence is called *Attiqa Qadisha*," the "Ancient Holy One," based on the depiction in Daniel 7 of God as *atiq yomin*, "the Ancient of Days." Elsewhere it is refered to as *Arikh Anpin*, the "long countenance," usually meaning the long-suffering or patient countenance of God. The pure and totally loving quality of this aspect of God is much emphasized, symbolized by

2. *Idra Rabba* is printed in Zohar 3:127b–145a; *Idra Zuta* in 3:287b–296b.

the white light that endlessly radiates from it. Next are the countenances of *Abba* and *Imma*, "Father" and "Mother," corresponding to
Hokhmah and *Binah* on the older chart, as could be predicted from symbols already associated with them. The following six *sefirot* are re-
configured into a single entity known as *Ze'ir Anpin*, the "short countenance" or impatient face of God. This is a black-bearded, "younger"
sort of male deity, as distinct from the white-bearded elder. (These two
male divine figures are based on an ancient Midrash that distinguished
between God's appearance to Israel as an "elder" at Sinai and as a
"youth" at the splitting of the sea.)[3] *Malkhut*, the tenth *sefirah*, is now the
fifth of the inner "faces" of God, here simply designated as *Nuqva*, "the
female." She is the female counterpart and mate of *Ze'ir Anpin*.

 This new language called for an intense focusing of the mystics' energies on the inner restoration of divinity. The situation of *Nuqva* was
seen as especially precarious, and all energies had to be marshaled toward the turning of *Ze'ir*'s attention to Her rescue. The rhythms of
shabbat and weekday are forgotten here; indeed little attention is given
to any of the conventional rubrics of prayer or worship through the
commandments. The Kabbalist is to focus rather on a somewhat bizarre
and highly anthropomorphic mental image of God's face, concentrat-
ing especially on the hairs of the divine beard. It is by means of pro
longed and uninterrupted meditation on these figures that the cosmic
energies leading to redemption are to be aroused.

 The symbolic language of the *Idrot* entered the "mainstream" of
kabbalistic discourse after its adoption by Rabbi Isaac Luria (1534–
1572) in a new version of Kabbalah that attained great popularity beginning in the late sixteenth century. There it was used in a highly messianic context, so much so that it has become difficult to distinguish
the Zohar's original *Idrot* from their use in the Lurianic setting. But it
does seem fair to say that the turn of Kabbalah toward a new magni-

---

3. Mekhilta Shirta 4 (ed. Horovitz-Rabin), p. 129.

fication of the messianic element, so characteristic of the sixteenth- and seventeenth-century developments, began in the *Idrot* themselves. Later Kabbalists, figures such as Rabbi Meir Ibn Gabbai and Rabbi Moses Cordovero, both of the sixteenth century as well, focus much more on the main body of the Zohar and remain at a relative distance from any sort of messianic activism.

Part IV

THE ZOHAR AS TEXT

16

Special Sections
of the Zohar

The main body of the Zohar constitutes about two thirds of the material included in the three volumes that are published as *Sefer ha-Zohar*. The Zohar literature, in the broader sense, encompasses these as well as two other volumes, *Tiqquney Zohar* and *Zohar Ḥadash*. Since it is generally accepted that *Tiqquney Zohar* and the *Ra'aya Meheimna* (published within *Sefer ha-Zohar*) are the work of a slightly later Kabbalist, we shall omit these two from our discussion of the Zohar and its sections; indeed, as they have been omitted from the current translation.

In addition to the main part of the Zohar, which we have already treated at length, there are a number of subcompositions of great importance within the Zohar. Because detailed outlines of the sections of the Zohar are readily available in the works of both Scholem and Tishby,[1] only the most important sections are discussed here.

Midrash ha-Ne'elam, or the "hidden" Midrash, is a separate composition covering the earlier sections of Genesis (through the Abraham narratives), the opening *parashah* of Exodus, and a few other small sec-

---

1. Gershom Scholem, *Major Trends in Jewish Mysticism*, pp. 159–63, Isaiah Tishby, *Wisdom of the Zohar*, v.1, pp. 1-7.

tions of the Torah. There is also *Midrash ha-Ne'elam* material in the *Zohar Ḥadash*, including sections on Ruth and the Song of Songs. Like the Zohar, the *Midrash ha-Ne'elam* consists of homilies on the Torah embedded within a narrative framework. Here the range of heroes is wider than in the main Zohar, including both earlier and later Talmudic sages. There is no concentration on Rabbi Shim'on or any particular group of teachers, although some special interest can be detected in Rabbi Yoḥanan ben Zakkai and his first-century disciples. Unlike the Zohar, the *Midrash ha-Ne'elam* was written largely in Hebrew, with something less than half of it shifting toward Aramaic.

The content and approach of the *Midrash ha-Ne'elam* are quite different from the rest of the Zohar literature. Sefirotic symbolism, the very basis of most Zoharic exegesis, is present only in partial form and is not employed with nearly the same range or skill as elsewhere in the Zohar. Instead, the *Midrash ha-Ne'elam* opts for more allegorical treatments of biblical themes, an approach hardly found in other parts of the Zohar.

Matnitin and *Tosefta* are brief nuggetlike passages scattered amid the pages of the Zohar. Their teachings almost always concentrate on the secrets of the *sefirot*, especially on the earliest stages of emanation. They are written in an especially obscure and mysterious-sounding Aramaic and are often difficult to understand.

Sitrei Torah, also scattered short passages throughout the Zohar, possibly reflects a transitionary document between *Midrash ha-Ne'elam* and the main body of the text. These passages include both allegorical treatments of the soul and discussion of the *sefirot*.

Sifra di-Tseni'uta is a single six-page treatise that constitutes the first revelation of the doctrine to be developed more fully in the *Idrot*. It takes the form of an anonymous commentary on the opening chapter of Genesis. Here, as in the *Matnitin*, the language is especially sonorous, impressive, and obscure.

Idra Rabbah and *Idra Zuta* have been discussed in the preceding section.

Heikhalot are two portions of the Zohar that deal with the "palaces" that lie below the *sefirot* in the Zohar's cosmology. These sections contain a good deal of the Zohar's unique angelology, very influential for later developments within Kabbalah. The second of these two passages also includes a description of the "seven palaces of defilement," demonic realms parallel to those of the sacred.

Special narrative-homilectical sections, essentially long digressions within the main Zohar text, are *Sava* ("the elder"), *Yanuqa* ("the child"), and *Rav Metivta* ("the academy master"). These are similar in form and content to the main body of the Zohar, if somewhat more elaborate in construction.

Zohar Hadash, (literally, the "new" Zohar) includes materials belonging to both the main body of the Zohar and the *Midrash ha-Ne'elam* that had been omitted from the original editions. This volume also contains commentaries on three of the "Five Scrolls," biblical books read liturgically in the course of the sacred year (surprisingly there is no Zohar to the Scroll of Esther, a text that is frequently treated elsewhere in the extant Zohar's pages), as well as additions to the *Tiqquney Zohar*.

17

The Question
of Authorship

The Zohar first appeared in Castile around the year 1290. Passages from
it are included in works by Castilian and Catalonian Kabbalists writing
at about that time. In some cases these are presented as quotations, attributed to "Yerushalmi" (usually referring to the Jerusalem Talmud, but
sometimes also to other works originating in the Holy Land), to Midrash, particularly "the Midrash of Rabbi Shim'on ben Yohai"; or to Zohar. Some scholars refer to it as an ancient work. In other cases, including passages in the writings of well-known Castilian Kabbalist Moses de
Leon and Barcelona author Baḥya ben Asher, pieces identical to sections of the Zohar are simply absorbed within other writings and presented as the authors' own. By the second decade of the fourteenth
century, the Zohar was referred to (by the author of *Tiqqunei Zohar*) as
a "prior" or completed document. Large portions of it were by then
available to such authors as David ben Judah he-Ḥasid, who paraphrased
and translated various sections, and Italian Kabbalist Menaḥem Recanati, who quoted copiously from the Zohar in his own commentary on
the Torah.

The question of the Zohar's origins has puzzled its readers ever since that first appearance, and no simple and unequivocal statement as to the question of its authorship can be made even in our own day. There is no question that the work was composed in the decades immediately preceding its appearance. It responds to literary works and refers to historical events that place it in the years following 1270. The 1280's seem like the most likely decade for composition of the main body of the Zohar, probably preceded by the *Midrash ha-Ne'elam* and possibly certain other sections. Indeed it is quite possible that the Zohar was still an ongoing project when texts of it first appeared, and that parts of it were being written even a decade later. Because the question of the Zohar's origins has been so hotly debated by readers and scholars over the centuries, it is important to offer a brief account here of the history of this discussion.

Debate about the Zohar's origins began in the decade of its first appearance. Fragments of the Zohar were first distributed by Rabbi Moses de Leon, who claimed that they were copied from an ancient manuscript in his possession. This was a classic technique of pseudepigraphy, the attribution of esoteric teachings to the ancients, to give them the respectability associated with hoary tradition. While some naive souls seem to have believed quite literally in the antiquity of the text and the existence of such a manuscript, others, including some of De Leon's fellow Kabbalists, joined in the pretense in order to heighten the prestige of these teachings. While they may have known that De Leon was the writer, and may even have participated in mystical conversations that were reflected in the emerging written text, they did believe that the *content* of the Zohar's teachings was indeed ancient and authentic. They probably saw nothing wrong in the creation of a grand literary fiction that provided for these ancient-yet-new teachings an elevated literary setting, one worthy of their profound truth. There were, however, skeptics and opponents of the Zohar right from the beginning, who depicted the whole enterprise as one of literary forgery.

Fascinating evidence of this early controversy is found in an account written by the Kabbalist Isaac of Acre, a wandering mystic who arrived in Castile in 1305. A manuscript version of Isaac's account was known to sixteenth-century chronicler Abraham Zacuto and was included in his *Sefer Yuḥasin*. Isaac tells us that he had already heard of the Zohar and came to Castile to learn more about it and specifically to investigate the question of the Zohar's origins. He managed to meet De Leon shortly before the latter's death. De Leon assured him that the ancient manuscript was real and offered to show it to him. By the time Isaac arrived at Avila, where De Leon had lived in the last years of his life, he had a chance only to meet the Kabbalist's widow. She denied that the manuscript had ever existed, recounting that her husband had told her that he was claiming ancient origins for his own work for pecuniary advantage. Others, however, while agreeing that there was no ancient manuscript source, claimed that De Leon had written the Zohar "through the power of the Holy Name." (This might refer either to some sort of trancelike "automatic writing" or to a sense that he saw himself as a reincarnation of Rabbi Shim'on and through the Name had access to his teachings.) Various other players then enter the account in a series of claims and counterclaims, and the text breaks off just before a disciple of De Leon is able to present what seems like promising testimony in the Zohar's behalf.

This account has been used by opponents of the Zohar and of Kabbalah in general in various attempts to dismiss the Zohar as a forgery and Moses de Leon as a charlatan. Most outspoken among these attempts is that of nineteenth-century historian Heinrich Graetz, for whom the Zohar was the epitome of the most lowly, superstitious element within medieval Judaism. Graetz and others assumed that the wife was the one who spoke the truth, with all other explanations serving to cover or justify the obvious chicanery of the author. Wanting to denigrate the Zohar, which did not fit the early modern enlightenment idea

of proper Judaism, Graetz did not consider the possibility that De Leon
might have told his wife such things for reasons other than their being
the simple truth. Sadly, her account may reflect the Kabbalist's assump-
tion of his wife's inability to appreciate his literary intentions. The claim
that he did it for the sake of selling books has about it the air of an explanation to a spouse, offered in a dismissive context.

Modern Zohar scholarship begins with the young Gershom Scholem's attempts to refute Graetz. He set out in the late 1920s to show
that the picture was more complex and that indeed there might be earlier layers to the Zohar. Awed by the vastness of the Zohar corpus, he
found it hard to believe that all of it could have been the work of a single author. But in a series of stunningly convincing essays Scholem re-
versed himself and came to the conclusion that the entire Zohar had
indeed been written by De Leon. He supported this conclusion by
careful analysis of the Zohar's language, its meager knowledge of the
geography of the Land of Israel, its relationship to philosophy and to
earlier works of Kabbalah, and its references to specific historical events
or dates. Most convincing was Scholem's painstaking philological analysis. He compared the Zohar's unique (and sometimes mistaken) use of
Aramaic linguistic forms to characteristic patterns of language found
(uniquely, he claimed) in De Leon's Hebrew works. Here he believed
he had found something of a literary fingerprint, making it finally clear
that De Leon was the author. As to the magnitude of the work and its
attribution to a single individual, Scholem was consoled by historical
parallels, particularly that of Jakob Boehme, a seventeenth-century German shoemaker, who had composed a vast corpus of writings under
the force of mystical inspiration.

But the matter is by no means ended here. The fact that Scholem
agreed with Graetz on the question of single authorship did not at all
mean that he shared in his lowly opinion of the Zohar or its author.
The parallel to Boehme in fact sounds rather like the writing "through

the power of the Holy Name" that had been suggested to Isaac of Acre. Assuming that Moses de Leon did write the entire Zohar, the question became one of understanding *how* this might be the case. Two specific questions come to the fore here. One concerns the notable differences between the Zohar's various sections. Could one person have written the *Midrash ha-Ne'elam*, with its hesitant, incomplete usage of sefirotic symbolism; the *Idrot*, where that symbolism has been incorporated and surpassed; and the obscure *matnitin* and *heikhalot*, along with the rich narrative and homilies of the main Zohar text? What can account for all these seeming variations in both literary style and symbolic content? The other question has to do with the intriguing relationship between a single author and the many voices that speak forth from the Zohar's pages. Is the community of mystics described here entirely a figment of the author's creative imagination? Is not some real experience of religious community reflected in the Zohar's pages? Might it be possible, to take an extreme view, that each of the speakers represents an actual person, a member of the Castilian Kabbalists' circle, here masked behind the name of an ancient rabbi? Or is there some other way in which the presence of many voices can be detected within the Zohar's pages?

Contemporary scholarship on the Zohar (here we are indebted especially to the pioneering work of Yehuda Liebes and its more recent development by Ronit Meroz) has parted company with Scholem on the question of single authorship. While it is tacitly accepted that De Leon did either write or edit long sections of the Zohar, including the main narrative-homiletical body of the text, he is not thought to be the only writer involved. Multiple layers of literary creativity can be discerned within the text. It may be that the Zohar should be seen as the product of a *school* of mystical practitioners and writers, one that could have existed even before 1270 and continued into the early years of the fourteenth century. Certain texts, including the *Midrash ha-Ne'elam* (perhaps an earlier recension of it than that which has survived?) belong to the oldest stratum of writing. The main part of the Zohar, including both the epic tale and the teachings of Rabbi Shim'on and his disciples, were indeed composed in the decades claimed by Scholem. Work on the Zohar did not cease, however, with the turn of the fourteenth century or the passing of Moses de Leon. In fact, the author of the *Tiqqunei Zohar* and the *Ra'aya Meheimna*, seen by Scholem as "later" addenda to the Zohar corpus, may represent the third "generation" of this ongoing school. It would have been in his day, and perhaps with the cooperation of several editors, that the fragments of the Zohar as first circulated were linked together into the somewhat larger units found in the surviving fourteenth- and fifteenth-century manuscipts.

There is no single, utterly convincing piece of evidence that has led scholars to this revision of Scholem's view. It is rather a combination of factors stemming from close readings of the text and from a body of scholarship on it that did not yet exist in Scholem's day. There is considerable evidence of what might be called "internal commentary" within the Zohar text. The "Secrets of the Torah" are an expansion of the brief and enigmatic *matnitin*, as the *Idrot* comment and enlarge upon themes first developed in the *Sifra di-Tseni'uta*. In the Zohar narrative there are also whole or partial stories that are told more than once, one version seemingly an expansion of an earlier recension. The same is true of certain homilies, some of which are repeated in part or whole several times within the text. While these could be explained as the developing project of a single author, they combine with ongoing consideration of the two questions just raised, the differing sections of the Zohar and the multiple "voices" that speak within the text, toward consideration of multiple or collective authorship. Historical evidence has shown that closed schools or societies (*havurot*) for various purposes were a common organizational form within Spanish Jewry. The image of Rabbi Shim'on and his followers encountering a series of mysterious teachers in the course of their wanderings looks rather like a possible description of a real such school encountering from outside its ranks various mystics who were accepted by the school's leader as legitimate teachers of secret Torah.

It is particularly intriguing to compare this hypothetical school of Kabbalists to another that is rather more clearly described in documents available to us. In neighboring Catalonia, the kabbalistic school of Naḥmanides lasted, side by side with his halakhic school, for three generations. Naḥmanides' disciple Shlomo ben Adret carried his master's teachings forward to a group of disciples who then wrote multiple commentaries on the secret aspects of Naḥmanides' work. That circle was significantly more conservative in its views of kabbalistic creativity than was the Castilian group. But we could easily imagine a parallel school of Castilian Kabbalists, beginning with the "Gnostics" of the mid-thirteenth century and extending forward over the same three generations, whose collective literary product, much freer and richer in imagination than the Naḥmanidean corpus, included the body of work finally edited into what later generations have come to know as the Zohar. It may indeed be that competition between these two schools of mystical thought played some role in the early stages of the editing process that finally resulted in the Zohar as we know it.

18

The Language
of the Zohar

The unique genius that finds expression in the Zohar has everything
to do with language. Its homiletical style builds on midrashic sensitivity to the nuances of biblical language and often seeks to go beyond it.
Underlying every page of the Zohar's reading of Torah is a rich "ear"
for associative links and plays on words, a constant search for "hints"
within the text that will allow for an opening to deeper levels of in
terpretation. This careful attention to the text is joined to the Zohar's
readiness to apply to it the symbolic language of the *sefirot*. It is the interplay between these two factors, heightened midrashic sensitivity and
the old-new grid of sefirotic symbols, that creates the unique and
powerful literary style of the Zohar.

Another element that plays a key role in the powerful impression
the Zohar has made on its readers throughout the generations is the
sonorous and seemingly mysterious Aramaic in which it was written.
All the sections of the Zohar, except for about half of *Midrash ha-
Ne'elam*, are written in Aramaic rather than Hebrew. While scholars
have devoted much attention to the unique grammatical and syntactical features of the Zohar's Aramaic, few have tried to understand *why*

the Zohar is written in Aramaic and what meaning this surprising choice of language might have had for the work's authors.

Aramaic was the spoken language of Jews, both in the Land of Israel and in Babylonia, from late biblical times (fourth to third century B.C.E.) until after the Islamic conquest and the replacement of Aramaic by Arabic (seventh century C.E.). The Talmud, in both its Babylonian and Palestinian versions, is composed mostly in Aramaic, as are portions of Midrash and other rabbinic writings. The Targum, existing in several versions, is the old Jewish translation of the Bible into Aramaic.

By the time the Zohar was written, Aramaic was a purely literary language for all but a tiny group of Jews in the mountains of Kurdistan. Knowledge of it elsewhere was purely passive, even among rabbinic scholars; only very rarely was a short treatise or poem still written in Aramaic. The choice to compose the Zohar in Aramaic gave to the work an anachronistic cast, and this immediately set the stage for its mysterious quality.

Some have claimed that the use of Aramaic was an attempt to write in the language of Rabbi Shim'on ben Yoḥai and his generation, thus adding a ring of authenticity to the Zohar's claim of antiquity. This is a rather difficult claim to press, however, since Rabbi Shim'on lived at the time of the Mishnah, in which his and his contemporaries' views are recorded in pure rabbinic Hebrew, the chief literary language for Jews in that Tannaitic period. Why would Rabbi Shim'on have written the Zohar in Aramaic? Certainly if he had set out to compose an *esoteric* work he would not have written it in the spoken vernacular, thus rendering it more rather than less accessible to unlettered Jews, from whose eyes the secrets were to be protected.

It would seem that we have to look to the effect of Aramaic on the Zohar's readers and writers rather than to the myth of Rabbi Shim'on to explain this surprising choice of language. In Spain of the thirteenth century, unlike Palestine of the second, Aramaic was indeed a mysterious and only vaguely understood language. Presenting secrets in Aramaic rather than Hebrew (a method that had been tried, in brief texts, before the Zohar) shrouded them in an obscuring veil, forcing a slower pace of reading upon those who delved into its pages. It also permitted a certain grandiloquence that might have seemed pretentious in the more familiar vehicle of medieval Hebrew. Images that might have been seen as trivial in Hebrew, especially if frequently repeated, maintained a certain mysterious grandeur when veiled by the obscurity of Aramaic dress.

The Zohar's Aramaic made the text significantly, but not impossibly, more difficult for the educated Jewish reader in its day. This was probably the precise intent: to offer the reader a sense that he had come to a more profound, and therefore less penetrable, sort of teaching. With some extra effort it would reveal to him the secret universe that the Zohar sought to share and pass on to its elite community of readers. Students of the Zohar come quickly to understand that the Aramaic of the Zohar was indeed a penetrable veil. The real difficulty in reading the text was of mastering the symbolic language and the subtlety with which it was employed.

It may also be that the Zohar's composition in Aramaic was not entirely a matter of conscious choice. Perhaps it was something that "happened," either in the author's psyche or in the community of mystics where the Zohar teachings were first shared orally. If there was a living community of Kabbalists in Castile in the 1280s, meeting by night in courtyards and gardens to study the secrets of the Torah, in what language did they share those secrets with one another? How did the transition take place from discussing the Hebrew text of Torah in Castilian, their only spoken language, back into Hebrew or Aramaic, for transcription onto the written page? Could it be that the rich sound of Aramaic, where each noun ended in a vowel, better reflected the sounds of their own Castilian speech than did Hebrew? Were they themselves somehow "seduced" by the mysterious sound of Aramaic to follow it into the fantasy realm represented by the Zohar?

These speculations may also be applied to the written text itself, especially if we assume that Rabbi Moses de Leon is the author of large portions of the Zohar. Some twenty Hebrew treatises of De Leon have survived, and several of these have now been published. Compared to the Zohar, they are relatively dull and uninspired. While the doctrinal content is very much the same, they possess little of the poetic muse and freedom of expression that so characterize the Zohar. One has the impression that De Leon stepped into another world when writing the Zohar, and that the transition from Hebrew to Aramaic was one of the ways he marked that portal. Working in this other, more dimly perceived language released his muse, as it were, giving him the freedom to soar to heights of imagination and literary excess that he would not have dared attempt in Hebrew. We might almost say that the use of Aramaic was some part of "the Holy Name" by which it was said that De Leon had written the Zohar.

The Aramaic of the Zohar is indeed a unique composite of dialects and features drawn from ancient literary sources. Details of Scholem's analysis of the Zohar's language can be found in his writings and need not be repeated here. Suffice it to say that the Zohar is a combination of Palestinian Aramaic, essentially the dialect of Targum Onkelos, with certain features, especially in the area of rhetorical terminology, that reflect the Babylonian Talmud. Various terms and usages of words in the Zohar clearly show the influence of medieval Hebrew, of interpretations (and sometimes misinterpretations) of Aramaic found in medieval Jewish dictionaries, and of the special vocabularly of medieval philosophy. A few Spanish terms have also been uncovered in the Zohar, although adequate research has not yet been done on the Zohar's language by scholars possessing a thorough knowledge of old Castilian.

What is surprising about this seemingly patched-together language is how well it works. There is a sense, as one reads the Zohar in the original, that the authors have created a linguistic vehicle that allows for great drama and passionate self-expression. That they did so with a limited vocabularly and a repertoire of few syntactical forms makes it all the more remarkable. Although technically one may say with Scholem that the Zohar's Aramaic is "artificial," not reflecting any known spoken dialect, in fact one who dwells for a while in the Zohar's pages finds it very much a *living* language, powerful and evocative in its own right.

A remarkable feature of the Zohar is the creation of new words that appear to be either Aramaic or perhaps typically Greek loan words in Aramaic garb but that in fact have no basis in any older text or language. These neologisms have given trouble to many an interpreter over the centuries, some of whom have sought to emend them in order to line them up with one Talmudic term or another. For reasons that are not clear, the majority of these words contain the "Q" sound, and often the "S," "F," or "T" as well. Perhaps their secret will be uncovered when the Zohar is studied in the context of its authors' spoken language. The current translation is particularly adept and creative in dealing with these linguistic inventions of the Zohar, as will be seen from the accompanying notes.

19

Editing and Printing
of the Zohar

One of the mysteries of the Zohar is the process by which it was edited and came to take the form in which we know it. All the manuscripts of the Zohar that predate its first printing (1558–60) are fragmentary, and there is reason to believe that the book was placed into its present form only by those who prepared it for printing. But the stages of the writing and editing process, reaching from the scattered quotations of Zohar materials found in the 1290s to the three grand volumes to come off the presses in Mantua (and the equally impressive one-volume counterpart in Cremona) some 270 years later, are difficult to trace.

The Zohar was identified as a *book* by the second decade of the fourteenth century. This is clear from references to it in the *Tiqqunei Zohar* and in other sources that quote it. But the extent or the exact contents of this book remain unknown. Just a bit later, around 1320, the Italian Kabbalist Menaḥem Recanati had access to large sections of the Zohar text, to which he referred copiously in his own works. Other fourteenth-century Kabbalists, such as David ben Judah he-Ḥasid (a grandson of Naḥmanides) and Shem Tov Ibn Gaon, also seem to have had only parts of the Zohar, and not the same parts as Recanati.

This probably indicates that variously organized collections of Zohar material were being circulated, each containing different parts of the written record. The surviving manuscripts that date to the fourteenth and fifteenth centuries correspond to these various quotations. Only rarely is there material in an early secondary source that does not appear in one or another manuscript and does not show up somewhere in the printed corpus of the Zohar. All this is to say that the editors, probably in the employ of the Italian printing houses, did their work well, including preparing much of the extant materials within the text.

That being the case, we have no good explanation of why the Zohar is so sparse in its treatment of the latter three books of the Torah, especially Deuteronomy, compared to the vast collections of material on Genesis and Exodus. Was the Zohar left incomplete possibly because of the death of Rabbi Moses de Leon? Did he or his circle simply run out of steam or lose interest in the project before its completion? Or does this seeming imbalance of materials have more to do with the editors at one stage or another than with the original authors?

Although Hebrew printing began in the 1470s, nearly a hundred years passed before the appearance of the Zohar. This is partly explained by a concern about making secrets too readily available, a concern shared by rabbinic authorities and some Kabbalists themselves. The dissemination of hand-copied manuscripts, few in number and costly to produce, could be much more carefully controlled than that of printed books. Kabbalah in the fifteenth century was still the esoteric doctrine of a small elite, and the ban on printing helped to keep it that. Only a few purely kabbalistic works were printed before the Zohar, Recanati's commentary on the Torah being the most prominent among them. The delay in printing may also mean, however, that there simply was no text appropriate for publication until that time. It is to the mostly anonymous mid-sixteenth-century editors that we owe a great debt of gratitude for the existence and preservation of the Zohar text.

The Mantua edition of the Zohar (dated 1558–1560 but possibly having followed the Cremona, 1560 edition in actual publication) opens with a letter of approbation by Rabbi Isaac De Lattes (d.c. 1570) permitting the printing of the Zohar. After reviewing the various rabbinic prohibitions against the public teaching and distribution of esoteric materials, De Lattes strongly urged that this policy be changed as messianic times drew near. Almost a third of the sixth millennium (that directly preceding and preparing the way for the seventh millennium or messianic age) had passed, he lamented, and only a wider knowledge of the Torah's secrets would stir Israel to do what was needed to effect redemption. This approbation has been reprinted in all later editions of the Zohar, despite the passage of centuries and the complex history of Jewry's messianic dreams. Printing of the Zohar opened the floodgates for the publication of various other kabbalistic works, issued first by various Italian printing houses in the 1560s and continuing from that time forward almost unceasingly to our own day.

As interest in Kabbalah continued to grow, another group of editors avidly sought manuscripts containing materials that had been omitted from the first editions. These efforts resulted in the *Zohar Ḥadash*, printed in Salonika in 1597. An Amsterdam printing of the main Zohar (1715) also added a significant number of variant readings to the text, cluttering the printed page but preserving some important manuscript sources. This Amsterdam text forms the basis of all later printed Zohar texts, including the very popular and widely reprinted Livorno (Leghorn) and Vilna editions.

Commentaries on the Zohar began to appear in the sixteenth century. Some of these (particularly the ones that did not devote their efforts to reinterpreting the Zohar to fit the later Lurianic Kabbalah) are very helpful in understanding the Zohar and occasionally also preserve a variant reading of the Zohar text. The largest and intellectually most significant of these is the *Or Yaqar* by Rabbi Moses Cordovero

(1522–1570). This vast *opus* has survived only in a single manuscript and has been published (in more than twenty volumes) only in the late twentieth century. But Cordovero was included in Abraham Azulai's seventeenth-century digest of Zohar commentaries *Or ha-Ḥammah*, and was influential in that more accessible form. Other significant commentaries include *Ketem Paz* by Rabbi Shim'on Lavi of Tripoli (sixteenth century) and *Miqdash Melekh* by Shalom Buzaglo of London (eighteenth century). The important twentieth-century editions are those of Reuben Margulies (*Mossad ha-Rav Kook*), with the most helpful source index *Nitsotsei Zohar*, and that of Yehudah Ashlag with the commentary *Ha-Sulam*. Ashlag's commentary is of the Lurianic variety and useful only for that purpose. He has also, however, translated the entire Aramaic text into Hebrew, a most important aid especially to the beginning student. More recent Hebrew renditions are found in two commentaries appearing in the 1990s, *Yedid Nefesh* and *Matoq mi-Devash*, as well as in a vocalized Zohar published by Yerid ha-Sefarim in 1998.

20

Influence and Canonization
of the Zohar

During the last two centuries of Jewish life in Spain, the Zohar continued to be copied and studied among small groups of devotees. It competed with two others schools of kabbalistic thought, the Catalonian and the Abulafian, for the attention of those few people interested in mystical pursuits. Some Kabbalists seem to have combined these various approaches, or else to have "migrated" in the course of their own quests from one school of mystical thought to another. Jewish rationalism was also very much alive in Spain through the fifteenth century, probably continuing to have a larger following than did Kabbalah. Manuscripts of Zohar fragments, increasingly compiled into longer sections of what we now recognize as "The Book Zohar," also reached Italy, the Byzantine lands of the Eastern Mediterranean, and the Holy Land during this period.

It was after the expulsion of Spanish Jewry in 1492 that the influence of Kabbalah entered a period of rapid growth. Some have attributed this to the suffering and despair that visited this once-proud group of Jewish communities in the period between 1391 and 1492. The devastation of the age, so it is said, caused Jews to seek out deeper resources of consolation than those offered by the typically optimistic worldview of the philosophers. The Lurianic Kabbalah of the late sixteenth century in particular has been read by Scholem and others as a reaction to the expulsion from Spain. This view has been disputed in more recent Kabbalah scholarship, notably by Moshe Idel.

Others claim that the growth of Kabbalah came as a response of a different sort to the Spanish expulsion. Jews throughout the Mediterranean world, including many Spanish exiles, were shocked and disgraced by the high numbers of Spanish Jews who converted to Christianity in the course of the fifteenth century. Once again the blame was placed partly at the door of philosophy. The intellectual sophistication of Spanish Jewry had supposedly led to a laxity in religious observance and a relative indifference to the question of religious identity. If ultimate truth lay with philosophy, it was said, one could wear the more convenient garb of the Christian rather than that of the hated and persecuted Jew while still believing in the same essential truths. Here again Kabbalah was brought forth as a weapon against such laxity and indifference to Jewish religious praxis.

Yet another view attributes the growth in Kabbalah's influence to the new home cultures in which former Iberian Jews found themselves. Ottoman Turkey of the sixteenth century was a welcoming haven for Jewish craft and mercantile skills. But it was not a good home for philosophical rationalism. The religious worldview of Turkey and the Near East, expressed both in Islam and in the Christianity of the region, was that of the closed *millet* system, with each faith community led by the sort of clergy who held fast to exclusive truth claims and total denigration of all outside influences. In this atmosphere it was precisely the closed-minded Zoharic view of the outside world that best served the community's needs, rather than the Aristotelian quasi-universalism of the philosophers, an ideology deriving from a very different time and place. A kabbalistic Judaism was better suited than was philosophy to

help Iberian Jews fit into and define themselves in the Ottoman context and in the spiritual universe of the Eastern Mediterranean.

Whatever the reason (and a combination of these factors is most
likely), new kabbalistic works were written and old ones were widely
distributed and explicated in the early sixteenth century. The Zohar
and other works of the Castilian tradition became especially prominent
in this period. Perhaps typical is the figure of Rabbi Meir Ibn Gabbai,
a Turkish Kabbalist who tells us that he was born in Spain in 1481 and
left as a child among the exiles. Ibn Gabbai's *magnum opus*, *Avodat ha-
Qodesh* (published in Venice in 1567) is a grand systematization of
Kabbalah and a defense of it against philosophy. Typically of scholars in
the sixteenth century, Ibn Gabbai knew a great many earlier texts and
sought to harmonize them with one another. But the great source of
kabbalistic truth was the Zohar, which Ibn Gabbai quotes on virtually
every page as "the Midrash of Rabbi Shim'on ben Yohai."

The kabbalistic conventicles of Safed, which flourished in the late-
sixteenth century, also accorded to the Zohar top place as the authoritative source of kabbalistic truth. Clearly the choice of Safed as a
place of settlement for Jews attached to the kabbalistic legacy had
much to do with its proximity to Meron, the supposed burial place of
Rabbi Shim'on ben Yohai. His tomb had been a site of pilgrimage for
local Jews much earlier, playing an important role in growth of the
Safed community. By the mid-sixteenth century it became a truly important shrine. Both Rabbi Moses Cordovero, who probably immi-
grated to Safed from elsewhere in the Ottoman realm, and Rabbi
Isaac Luria, who came from Egypt, chose to live in Safed because of
the nearness of holy graves and the possibility (described by Cordovero in his *Sefer Gerushin*) of achieving mystical knowledge through
prostration upon them. Among the sacred dead of the Galilee, Rabbi
Shim'on, now acclaimed as the undisputed author of the Zohar, took
a central place. Luria specifically hoped to achieve a true understand-

ing of passages in the Zohar by visiting what he believed to be the grave of its author.

The "return" of Kabbalah to the Galilean landscape of the Zohar's heroes fired the imagination of Jews throught the diaspora. Reports of the holy men of Safed, especially the mysterious figure of Luria, known as ha-ARI ha-Qadosh ("the holy lion"), were widely copied and printed in several versions. A vast literature of both kabbalistic writings and ethical or pietistic works influenced by Kabbalah poured forth from the printing presses of Venice, Constantinople, and Amsterdam, to be distributed throughout the Jewish world. It did not take long until the claim emerged that the soul of the ARI was in fact a reincarnation of Rabbi Shim'on ben Yoḥai.

It was in this period that the Zohar came to be considered not only an ancient and holy book but also a *canonical* text, bearing authority comparable to that of the Bible and the Talmud. The authority of the Zohar as the prime source of mystical truth had already been considered by fourteenth-century Kabbalists, some of whom came to view its words as superior to those of Naḥmanides, for example, because of its allegedly greater antiquity. Naḥmanides was portrayed by these writers as a "modern" source, whose word could be set aside by a contrary quotation from the work of Rabbi Shim'on ben Yoḥai. But in the sixteenth century it was said that Elijah himself had appeared to Rabbi Shim'on, and the Zohar's authority became that of heaven itself. Meir Ibn Gabbai traced the kabbalistic tradition back to Sinai, claiming that Zoharic secrets were given to Moses along with the written Torah.

Canonical status, in the context of Judaism, potentially bears within it halakhic authority as well as mystical prestige. If the Zohar contained the "true" meaning of both written and oral Torah, might it be used as a source of legal authority, especially in ritual and liturgical matters, as well? This question came up among halakhic scholars, especially in a select few cases in which the Zohar seemed to contradict the majority opinion of rabbis deciding the law on the basis of Talmudic precedent and its formulation in the literature of responsa and codes. In fact, as scholars have shown, these cases mostly turn on local custom, with the Zohar reflecting either Franco-German or old Spanish customs, while the *halakhah* had decided in favor of other customs. A classic example of such halakhic dispute involving the Zohar concerns the donning of *tefillin* on the intermediate weekdays of Passover and *Sukkot*. The Zohar expresses itself strongly on the issue, considering the wearing of *tefillin* on those days an insult to the festival and a virtual sacrilege. Although the halakhic codes mostly tended otherwise, some halakhic authorities bowed to the Zohar, and the use of *tefillin* on those days was rejected throughout the Sephardic (and later Hasidic) communities.

Thanks to the influence of the Safed revival of mystical studies, Kabbalah became widely known among Eastern European Jews in the seventeenth century. The works of Rabbi Isaiah Horowitz, a Prague Kabbalist who later settled in Jerusalem, carried the teachings of Ibn Gabbai and Cordovero, among others, to preachers throughout the Ashkenazic communities. Here too the Zohar was widely quoted. Prayerbooks with kabbalistic commentaries, including those by Cordovero and Horowitz, brought kabbalistic thinking into the realm of actual synagogue practice. The highly mythical Kabbalah of Naftali Bacharach, seventeenth-century German author of *Emeq ha-Melekh* ("Valley of the King"), is primarily influenced by the language and imagery of the Zohar.

Another area of the growing canonicity of the Zohar is its use in liturgical contexts and its appearance in digests of daily religious practice. Various kabbalistic *Tiqqunim*, or "Orders," were published throughout the seventeenth and eighteenth centuries. These included many collections of Zohar passages to be recited during the night vigils of *Shavu'ot* and *Hosha'na Rabbah*, at the Sabbath table, and on various other occasions. It came to be understood in this period that recitation of the oral Zohar was efficacious even for those who did not understand its meaning. In the nineteenth century, vocalized editions of the Zohar were printed to facilitate this practice and to ensure that the recitation would nevertheless be performed with some degree of accuracy. Various digests were also produced for daily study and recitation, especially in the eighteenth century. The most widespread of these was called *Ḥoq le-Yisra'el* (published in Cairo in 1740), including passages to be recited each day from the Torah, the Prophets, the Hagiographia, Mishnah, the Talmud, the Zohar, ethical guides, and legal decisors. The *Ḥemdat Yamim*, an anonymous compendium of kabbalistic praxis (published in Izmir in 1731–1732), prescribes readings from the Zohar for nearly every conceivable occasion in the Jewish liturgical year. In both of these compendia we see the Zohar at the apex of its acceptance and integration into the daily regimen of Jewish spiritual life.

In the late seventeenth and early eighteenth centuries, the messianic movement around Sabbatai Tsevi (1626–1676) swept through the Jewish communities. In the more radical forms of Sabbatianism, the place of the Zohar became even greater as the authority of Talmudic law came to be questioned. The kabbalistic system of Nathan of Gaza (c. 1643–1680), the great prophet of Sabbatianism, is based on the imagery of the Zohar, and devotion to the Zohar was touted loudly throughout the history of Sabbatianism. Some of the later Ashkenazic Sabbatians, followers of Jacob Frank, came to refer to themselves as "Zoharites," Jews who followed the authority of the Zohar while rejecting that of the Talmud and the rabbis. This would of course be a spurious claim had the authors of the Zohar been asked their opinion, because they had no intention of rebelling against Talmudic authority. But by this time (and in these circles) the Zohar was being read through the lenses of such radical interpreters as the *Ra'aya Meheimna*, the fifteenth-century *Sefer ha-Kanah*, the anonymous work *Galei Razayya*, and the writings of Nathan of Gaza. When seen as the font of this literary tradition, the Zohar could be read as a very radical work indeed.

The decline of Sabbatianism in the mid-eighteenth century preceded by only a few decades the beginning of the Enlightenment era in Western Europe and the admission of Jews into a more open and religiously tolerant society. As large numbers of Jews became eager supporters of what they could see only as emancipation, readings of Judaism that supported or fit this new situation became widespread. One feature of this emerging postenlightenment Judaism, whether in its reform or orthodox versions, was either an open rejection or a quiet setting aside of Kabbalah and of the Zohar in particular. Scholem wrote an essay about several obscure nineteenth-century figures whom he designated as "The Last Kabbalists in Germany." We have already spoken of Heinrich Graetz's negative views of the Zohar, a position that was widely shared by his contemporaries. While there were a few scholars in the period of the *Wissenschaft des Judentums* (Adolf Jellinek of Vienna is the most notable) who studied the Zohar, it was mostly neglected by westernized Jews throughout the nineteenth and early twentieth centuries.

In Eastern Europe the situation was quite different. Hasidism, a popular religious revival based on Kabbalah, continued to revere the Zohar and believe in its antiquity. Several significant Zohar commentaries were written within Hasidic circles, and the authors of Hasidic works often referred to the Zohar. Rabbi Pinhas of Korzec, an early Hasidic master, was said to have thanked God that he was born after the appearance of the Zohar, "for the Zohar kept me a Jew." Hasidic legend has it that when the Zohar was published by his sons, who owned the printing works in Slawuta, they dipped the press in the *mikveh* ("ritual bath") before printing each volume, so great was the holy task that was about to come before it. Hasidic masters, because of this legend, went out of their way to acquire copies of the Slawuta edition of the Zohar and to study from it. The great opponent of Hasidism, Rabbi Elijah (the "Gaon") of Vilna (1720–1797) was also a Kabbalist, and within the circle of his disciples there was a small group that continued the study of Zohar for several generations.

Among the Sephardic Jews, the reputation of the Zohar as a holy book was particularly strong. Jews in such far-flung communities as Morocco, Turkey, and Iraq studied it avidly. Simple Jews recited the Zohar much in the way that uneducated East European Jews recited the Psalms. Beginning in the eighteenth century, Jerusalem became known as a center of kabbalistic studies, and Jews from throughout these communities went there and studied works that emanated from that center. Among Sephardic Jews it was primarily the Lurianic Kabbalah that held sway, and the Zohar, while revered, was generally viewed through the Lurianic prism. Only as enlightenment ideas began to spread in the early twentieth century, partly through the arrival of European Jews in the Colonial era, was the authority of the Zohar questioned.

The writings of Scholem, Tishby, and the scholars following in their wake have done much to make the Zohar intelligible to moderns and to renew interest in its study. Tishby's *Wisdom of the Zohar*, which translated selected passages from Aramaic into Hebrew, was a highly successful attempt to make the Zohar more accessible to an educated Israeli readership. The interest aroused among scholars of religion by Scholem's highly readable and insightful essays, especially those first presented at the Eranos conferences, served to kindle great interest in Kabbalah within the broader scholarly community. This interest is maintained today thanks to the profound and sometimes provocative studies of Yehuda Liebes, Elliot Wolfson, and others. The important writings of Moshe Idel continue to bring many aspects of Kabbalah to the attention of the scholarly and intellectual world. The availability of English and other translations, including the selections in Tishby and anthologies by both Scholem and Matt, have also served the Zohar well in creating readerships outside of Israel. In more recent decades this intellectual interest in Kabbalah has spread to wider circles, including many interested in questions of symbolism, philosophy of language, and related issues.

At the same time, two other seemingly unrelated phenomena have come together to increase greatly the interest in Zohar studies at the turn of the twenty-first century. One is the broad interest throughout the Western world in works of mysticism and "spirituality." Our age has seen a great turn toward sources of wisdom neglected by two or three centuries of modernity, partly in hope of finding in them a truth that will serve as a source of guidance for the difficult and complex times in which we live. Recently interest in the Zohar and Kabbalah has emerged as part of this trend. As is true of all the other wisdoms examined in the course of this broad cultural phenomenon, the interest in Kabbalah includes both serious and trivial or "faddist" elements. This revival of Kabbalah is a complicated phenomenon, containing expressions of great hunger for religious experience and personal growth, alongside the broader quest for wisdom. Types of thought once set aside as "irrational" and views of the universe dismissed as "unscientific" are now being reexamined as reflections of deeper aspects of the human spirit, creations stemming from a realm of mind that reason itself cannot comprehend.

This interest has come to be combined with a very different revival of Kabbalah, primarily in Israel, after the 1967 and 1973 wars. It is manifest in the growth of kabbalistic *yeshivot*, or academies; by the publication of many new editions of kabbalistic works; and by a campaign of public outreach intended to spread the teachings of Kabbalah more broadly. This new emphasis on Kabbalah is partly due to the reassertion of pride in the Sephardic heritage, where Kabbalah has an important place. It is also in part related to the difficult and trying times through which Israel has lived, resulting in both a resurgence of messianism and a turn to "practical Kabbalah," a longstanding part of Near Eastern Judaism, as a source of protection against enemies and hope of victory over them. The Kabbalah taught in these circles is primarily of the Lurianic variety, as interpreted through a long chain of Jerusalem-based teachers. Some versions of what is proferred as "Kabbalah" today can be described only as highly debased renditions of the original teachings and include large elements of folk religion that have little to do with actual kabbalistic teachings. But the Zohar, even if reinterpreted in Lurianic terms, even when enshrined more than it is comprehended, is revered throughout these circles as the primary font of kabbalistic truth, the ancient teaching of Rabbi Shim'on ben Yoḥai.

How this very complex interweaving of forces will affect the future of interest in Kabbalah is yet to be seen. It is certain, however, that the Zohar will continue to find a place in the hearts of new readers, some of whom will turn to the more authentic and profound aspects of its teachings. It is hoped that these readers will be helped and guided by this *Guide* as they turn to study the holy Zohar in its most recent translation and commentary.

Bibliography

The following list includes important studies of the Zohar beginning with the writings of Gershom Scholem. Insights found throughout these studies have helped to shape this *Guide*. (H) indicates that the study is written in Hebrew.

Abrams, Daniel. "When Was the Introduction to the Zohar Written and Changes Within Differing Copies of the Mantua Printing." *Asufot* 8 (1994): 211–26. (H)

Brody, Seth. "Human Hands Dwell in Heavenly Heights: Worship and Mystical Experience in Thirteenth-Century Kabbalah." Doctoral dissertation, University of Pennsylvania, 1991.

———. "Human Hands Dwell in Heavenly Heights: Contemplative Ascent and Theurgic Power in Thirteenth-Century Kabbalah." In *Mystics of the Book: Themes, Topics, and Typologies*. Ed. R. Herrera. New York: Peter Lang, 1993.

Farber-Ginat, Asi. "On the Sources of Rabbi Moses De Leon's Early Kabbalistic System." *Jerusalem Studies in Jewish Thought* 3 (1983–84): 67–96. (H)

Gottlieb, Ephraim. *The Kabbalah in the Writings of Rabbi Bahya ben Asher Ibn Halawa*. Jerusalem: Kiryath Sefer, 1970. (H)

———. *Studies in the Kabbalah Literature*. Ed. J. Hacker. Tel Aviv: Tel Aviv University, 1976. (H)

Green, Arthur. *Keter: The Crown of God in Early Jewish Mysticism.* Princeton: Princeton University Press, 1997.

———. "Shekhinah, the Virgin Mary, and the Song of Songs." *AJS Review* 26:1 (2002): 1–52.

Grözinger, Karl, "Tradition and Innovation in the Concept of Poetry in the Zohar." *Jerusalem Studies in Jewish Thought* 8 (1989): 347–86. (H)

Gruenwald, Itamar. "From Talmudic to Zoharic Homiletics." *Jerusalem Studies in Jewish Thought* 8 (1989): 255–98. (H)

Hellner-Eshed, Melila. "A River Issues Forth from Eden: The Language of Mystical Invocation in the Zohar." *Kabbalah* 3 (1998): 287–310. (H)

———. "Do Not Stir Up or Awaken My Love Until It Pleases: The Language of Awakening in the Zohar." *Kabbalah* 5 (2000): 327–52. (H)

———. "The Language of Mystical Experience in the Zohar: The Zohar Through Its Own Eyes." Doctoral dissertation, Hebrew University, 2001. (H)

Huss, Boaz. "*Sefer ha-Zohar* as a Canonical, Sacred, and Holy Text: Changing Perspectives on the Book of Splendor Between the Thirteenth and Eighteenth Centuries." *Journal of Jewish Thought and Philosophy* 7 (1998): 257–307.

———. "A Sage Is Preferable to a Prophet: Rabbi Simeon bar Yohai and Moses in the Zohar." *Kabbalah* 4 (1999): 103–39. (H)

———. "Holy Place, Holy Time, Holy Book: The Influence of the Zohar on Pilgrimage Rituals to Meron and the Lag be-Omer Festival." *Kabbalah* 7 (2002): 237–56. (H)

Idel, Moshe. "The Concept of the Torah in Heikhalot Literature and Its Metamorphoses in Kabbalah." *Jerusalem Studies in Jewish Thought* 1 (1981): 23–84. (H)

———. "Sefirot Above Sefirot." *Tarbiz* 51 (1982): 239–80. (H)

———. "Kabbalistic Material from Rabbi David ben Yehudah he-Hasid's School." *Jerusalem Studies in Jewish Thought* 2 (1983): 169–207. (H)

———. "The World of Angels in Human Shape." In *Studies in Jewish Mysticism, Philosophy, and Ethical Literature Presented to Isaiah Tishby*. Jerusalem: Magnes Press, 1986, pp. 1–66. (H)

———. *Kabbalah: New Perspectives*. New Haven: Yale University Press, 1988.

———. "Sexual Images and Acts in Kabbalah." *Zemanim* 42 (1992): 31–39. (H)

Kadari, Menahem Z. *A Grammar of Zohar Aramaic*. Jerusalem: Kirjath Sefer, 1971. (H)

Katz, Jacob. *Halakhah and Kabbalah: Studies in the History of Jewish Religion*. Jerusalem: Magnes Press, 1984. (H)

Liebes, Yehuda. "Sections of the Zohar Lexicon." Doctoral dissertation, Hebrew University, 1976. (H)

———. "The Messiah of the Zohar." In *The Messianic Idea in Jewish Thought*. Jerusalem: Israel Academy of Sciences and Humanities, 1982, pp. 87–234. (H)

———. "How the Zohar Was Written" *Jerusalem Studies in Jewish Thought* 8 (1989): 1–72. (H)

———. *Studies in the Zohar*. Albany: State University of New York Press, 1993.

———. "Zohar and Eros." *Alpayyim* 9 (1994): 67–119. (H)

———. "The Zohar as a Halakhic Work." *Tarbiz* 64 (1995): 581–605. (H)

———. "Zohar as Renaissance." *Da'at* 46 (2001): 5–11. (H)

Matt, Daniel C. "*Matnita Dilan*: A Technique of Innovation in the Zohar." *Jerusalem Studies in Jewish Thought* 8 (1989): 123–46. (H)

———. "New-Ancient Words: The Aura of Secrecy in the Zohar." In *Gershom Scholem's 'Major Trends in Jewish Mysticism': 50 Years After*. Ed. P. Schäfer and J. Dan. Tübingen: Mohr, 1994.

Meroz, Ronit. "Zoharic Narratives and Their Adaptations." *Hispania Judaica Bulletin* 3 (2000): 3–63.

———. "The Chariot of Ezekiel: An Unknown Zoharic Commentary." *Te'uda* 16/17 (2001): 567–616. (H)

————. "'And I Was Not There?': The Complaints of Rabbi Shimon bar Yohay According to an Unknown Story of the Zohar." *Tarbiz* 71 (2002): 163–93. (H)
————. "The Path of Silence: An Unknown Zoharic Story." Forthcoming. (H)
————. *The Pearl, the Fish, and the Matza: The Spiritual Biography of Rashby.* Jerusalem: Mosad Bialik, forthcoming. (H)
Oron, Michal. "Kol ha-Neshamah Tehalel Yah: An Allegorical Expression of the Concept of Death in the Zohar." *Dapim le-Mehqar be-Sifrut* 4 (1988): 8–35. (H)
———— "Artistic Elements in the Homiletics of the Zohar." *Jerusalem Studies in Jewish Thought* 8 (1989): 299–310. (H)
————. "'Set Me as a Seal upon Your Heart': Studies in the Poetics of the Zohar's Author in *Sava de-Mishpatim.*" In *Massu'ot: Studies in Kabbalistic Literature and Jewish Philosophy in Memory of Prof. Ephraim Gottlieb.* Ed. M. Oron and A. Goldreich. Jerusalem: Mosad Bialik , 1994, pp. 1–24. (H)
Scholem, Gershom. "Did Rabbi Moses De Leon Write the Zohar?" *Mada'ey ha-Yahadut* 1 (1926): 16–29. (H)
————. "Questions on Zohar Criticism Based upon Its Knowledge of the Land of Israel." *Zion* 1 (1925): 40–56. (H)
————. *Major Trends in Jewish Mysticism.* New York: Schocken Books, 1941.
Ta-Shma, Israel. "On the Literary Sources of the Zohar." *Tarbiz* 60 (1991): 663–65. (H)
————. *Ha-Nigle she-Banistar: The Halachic Residue in the Zohar.* Tel Aviv: Hakibbutz Hameuchad, 1995. (H)
————. "Additional Inquiries into the Problem of Ashkenazi Sources to the Zohar." *Kabbalah* 5 (2000a): 353–58. (H)
————. "More on the Ashkenazic Origins to the Zohar." *Kabbalah* 3 (1998): 259–64; and 5 (2000b): 353–58. (H)
Wolfson, Elliot E. "Left Contained in the Right: A Study in Zoharic Hermeneutics." *AJS Review* 11:1 (1986): 27–52.
————. "The Hermeneutics of Visionary Experience: Revelation as Interpretation in the Zohar." *Religion* 18 (1988a): 311–45.
————. "Light Through Darkness: The Ideal of Human Perfection in the Zohar." *Harvard Theological Review* 81:8 (1988b): 73–95.
————. "The Anthropomorphic and Symbolic Image of the Letters in the Zohar." *Jerusalem Studies in Jewish Thought* 8 (1989): 147–82. (H)
————. "Beautiful Maiden Without Eyes: *Peshat* and *Sod* in Zoharic Hermeneutics." In *The Midrashic Imagination.* Ed. M. Fishbane. Albany: State University of New York Press, 1993, pp. 155–203.
————. "Forms of Visionary Ascent as Ecstatic Experience in the Zoharic Literature." In *Gershom Scholem's 'Major Trends in Jewish Mysticism': 50 Years After.* Ed. P. Schäfer and J. Dan. Tübingen: Mohr, 1994a.
————. *Through a Speculum That Shines: Vision and Imagination in Medieval Jewish Mysticism.* Princeton: Princeton University Press, 1994b.